What people are

Pray Wait Trust

"Simon writes like a trusted friend, relatable and real, who is not simply *talking* to us but *walking* with us. *Pray, Wait Trust* is such a timely book. It brings words of encouragement and hope for those unexpected seasons of uncertainty, and fresh confidence and faith for the journey ahead."

Chris Cartwright, general superintendent, Elim churches

"Nobody is immune from tough seasons in life, but many of us struggle to navigate these challenging times. Simon has written a book that is both biblical and incredibly practical. Personally, his words resonated deeply with me, and I feel this book will become an essential toolkit for many as we travel courageously along the most uncertain paths in life."

Cathy Madavan, speaker, broadcaster and author

"Pray, wait and trust are definitely principles we need to learn to live by as Christians. My good friend Simon has authentically brought these to life through his own story and insights into scripture. I found this book a real encouragement, and I know you will too."

Rev Mark Greenwood, national evangelist and head of evangelism, Elim Churches UK

"Simon's excellent book is both personal and practical. From his own experience, he provides a guidebook for those who make the discovery that life rarely works out how they had hoped or planned. Simon shows us how to not just survive those seasons of frustration, but to thrive in them, as we intentionally draw close to God and learn to lean on Him."

Rev Duncan Clark, senior minister, Coventry Elim Church

"Simon Lawton's latest book has all the hallmarks that made his previous publications such a help to so many. The author, in a very clear and compelling manner, sets out the scriptural basis for the principles set out in the book's title. What makes this work so compelling, however, is not just the author's powers of description or dexterity in handling scripture; Simon has lived out these principles in recent times and discovered first hand that this ancient revelation is as reliable in twenty-first century life as it was when first given by God."

Rev James Glass, elim regional leader, Scotland and Northwest England

"*Pray, Wait, Trust* is an honest, accessible, practical and encouraging road map to guide us when life takes an unexpected turn. This book is not theory, but was born out of a time of difficulty in the author's life. It is packed full of wisdom, honesty & lots of scripture to help the reader cope with life's curveballs. I wholeheartedly recommend it!"

Rev Steve Ball, elim regional leader, Wales and Southern England

"Simon's book invites us into the mystery of prayer and encounter. It is a vivid and beautiful reminder that God is waiting for us to listen to Him, to walk with Him, to worship Him. It is also a call to the fundamental reality that God has invited us to walk with Him, to sit with Him and to love Him. This wonderful book is a raw reminder that when we seek God with all our heart, we will find Him."

Malcolm Duncan (FRSA), pastor, author, theologian, broadcaster

PRAY
WAIT
TRUST

What to do when life throws you a curveball

SIMON LAWTON

ISBN 978 1 9996489 6 1

e-ISBN 978 1 9996489 7 8

First edition 2023

Acknowledgments

Scripture quotations are primarily taken from the Holy Bible, New International Version Anglicised. Copyright ā 1979, 1984, 2011 Biblica, formerly International Bible Society. Used by permission of Hodder & Stoughton Ltd, an Hachette UK company. All rights reserved. "NIV" is a registered trademark of Biblica. UK trademark number 1448790.

Scripture quotations marked 'AMP' are taken from the Amplified® Bible Copyright © 2015 by The Lockman Foundation. Used by permission.

Scripture quotations marked 'ESV' are taken from the ESV® Bible (The Holy Bible, English Standard Version®). ESV® Text Edition: 2016. Copyright © 2001 by Crossway, a publishing ministry of Good News Publishers. The ESV® text has been reproduced in

A catalogue record for this book is available from the British Library

Contents

Introduction

There are moments in all our lives when we are thrown an unexpected curveball; when we simply don't understand what God is doing and have no idea what to do next.

I remember watching the Omaha Royals baseball team while visiting family in Nebraska, and being struck by the speed at which the pitcher threw the ball. It's quite an art! Every so often the pitcher will throw a slower ball that curves downward before reaching the home plate. The unexpected movement and slower pace are intended to catch the batter out and set him off balance. The curveball pitch is so well known in American culture that the phrase has become a common expression that means "something that is unexpected and difficult to deal with".

Our journeys through life often throw us unexpected curveballs. There will be seasons when we feel as if we have our lives under control and everything appears to be going well, but then suddenly everything spins out of control. It's important to remember that while these curveballs are surprising to us, they are not a surprise to God. In fact, we could say that they are allowed and used by God for His purposes.

In the middle of the pandemic, I resigned my position as senior pastor of the church I was leading in the Midlands. Sadly, things had not worked out as we had anticipated – it just happens that way sometimes. However, it was undoubtedly the right thing to do, and I have never for one moment regretted the decision.

But what kind of crazy person does that? My resignation also resulted in my wife losing her job, because she was working alongside me at the church. We literally went from having two salaries to none. We hadn't anticipated the start of a second lockdown in the UK either, and there being little or no opportunity of a new church to lead as a result.

Over the next fourteen months we went through what I can only describe as a wilderness experience. Having lost my American birth father the previous year, I experienced the loss of my lovely aunt and my beloved adopted dad within five months of each other, shortly followed by the death of our little black dog, who sadly came to the end of his seventeen years on planet earth (dog owners will understand just how devastating this is for the whole family!).

We had very little regular income during this period, and we were also experiencing the anxiety of the pandemic, the monotony of endless lockdown life and the limitations this was having on our normal daily lives. Like many others, I had moments of doubt, fear and anxiety about the future. I wondered what God was up to. What was His plan for our lives? *Where are you, Lord?* I experienced days when discouragement, despair and disillusionment stalked me. I felt like we'd lost everything. I experienced moments of restlessness, but also long periods of indescribable peace. Ministry opportunities came and went. Nothing seemed right.

Thankfully, as I write this, I'm almost through my second year of leading a wonderful church in Banbury, Oxfordshire. We are so blessed, but we had to endure a season of praying, waiting and trusting before we experienced the blessing.

The words from Lamentations below totally reflected how I felt at the time: pretty much at rock bottom, yet not without hope:

I'll never forget the trouble, the utter lostness, the taste of ashes, the poison I've swallowed. I remember it all – oh, how well I remember – the feeling of hitting the bottom. But there's one other thing I remember, and remembering, I keep a grip on hope: God's loyal love couldn't have run out, his merciful love couldn't have dried up. They're created new every morning. How great your faithfulness! I'm sticking with God (I say it over and over). He's all I've got left. God proves to be good to the man who passionately waits, to the woman who diligently seeks. It's a good thing to quietly hope, quietly hope for help from God. It's a good thing when you're young to stick it out through the hard times. (Lamentations 3:19-27, MSG)

I have no idea what you're facing right now...

It could be the loss of a precious loved one, the end of a cherished relationship, a job loss or sudden change in your work situation, a loss of income or livelihood. Perhaps you feel frustrated by the situation you have found yourself in, with no sign of it coming to an end. Or perhaps everything you have built or been working towards appears to have been dismantled. Perhaps your health has taken a turn for the worse and the future looks bleak right now.

For some, everything changes in a single moment. All of a sudden everything is different. People say that life is full of surprises, and it is – but not all of them are pleasant ones. Some leave us absolutely devastated, not knowing which way to turn. My heart goes out to you if this applies to you. You've probably realised that life will never be the same again. However, the God of hope always has a plan... and it's a good one. While we don't fully understand His ways or what He allows to happen, He is the God who promises to work all things for the good of those who love Him (see Romans 8:28).

Perhaps as you're reading this you are full of fear, anxiety and uncertainty about the future. You're waiting for God to intervene, to reveal His hand, to bring breakthrough, to open that door, to heal your body, to provide what you need or to answer your prayers. Although it's unlikely that our lives have been as challenging as Paul's, His words do resonate and bring encouragement:

We carry this precious Message around in the unadorned clay pots of our ordinary lives. That's to prevent anyone from confusing God's incomparable power with us. As it is, there's not much chance of that. You know for yourselves that we're not much to look at. We've been surrounded and battered by troubles, but we're not demoralized; we're not sure what to do, but we know that God knows what to do; we've been spiritually terrorized, but God hasn't left our side; we've been thrown down, but we haven't broken. (2 Corinthians 4:7-9, MSG)

Where are you, God?

"I am worn out calling for help; my throat is parched. My eyes fail, Looking for my God" (Psalms 69:3).

Life can be very challenging at times. God may appear silent or even absent. The psalmist reminds us we're in good company, as he felt the same way on many occasions. Praying can become difficult in those seasons. Hearing God's voice personally can seem harder

xiv

still. The wilderness may feel like it's become your constant abode, and perhaps none of what is happening appears to make any sense. "Where are you in all this, Father? What are you saying to me?"

Silence.

So how should we respond when life throws us a curveball? How do we respond to the sudden changes in our circumstances, when life no longer makes sense?

Pray, wait, trust

The day after I resigned from my position as pastor, I saw a meme on Instagram. It simply said: "Pray. Wait. Trust." I was captivated by its powerful simplicity, and was determined to hold on to it. Two months later, when Julia and I were struggling and feeling more than a little anxious about our situation, and worrying about how we would put food on the table, I was reminded of this image and its simple words. As I shared it with Julia again, I became aware of the incredible peace of God filling the room and our hearts. In that moment, I knew that His desire for us in this season was to PRAY, WAIT, TRUST.

This is something the writer to the Hebrews identified:

"For this is the hope of our salvation. But hope means that we must trust and wait for what is still unseen. For why would we need to hope for something we already have? So, because our hope is set on what is yet to be seen, we patiently keep on waiting for its fulfilment. And in a similar way, the Holy Spirit takes hold of us in our human frailty to empower us in our weakness. For example, at times we don't even know how to pray, or know the best things to ask for. But the Holy Spirit rises up within us to super-intercede on our behalf, pleading to God with emotional sighs too deep for words. God, the searcher of the heart, knows fully our longings, yet he also understands the desires of the Spirit, because the Holy Spirit passionately pleads before God for us, his holy ones, in perfect harmony with God's plan and our destiny. So we are convinced that every detail of our lives is continually woven together for good, for we are his lovers who have been called to fulfill his designed purpose. For he knew all about us before we were born, and he destined us from the beginning to share the likeness of his Son." (Romans 8:24-29, TPT)

Our season of praying, waiting and trusting lasted nearly fourteen months, but it seemed much longer! There were many long, difficult, monotonous days, and moments when I almost felt I'd lost my call to ministry – even wondering whether I should look for a new career. My confidence was smashed. Doubts and fears arose, along with the constant question in my heart: "Where are you, God, and what are you doing in all this?"

No guarantee of immunity

Being a Christian doesn't make us immune from life's problems. Job lived an exemplary life, yet he lost everything: family, homes and income. Even his health deteriorated. He cried:

"God has blocked my way so that I cannot pass; he has shrouded my paths in darkness. He has stripped me of my honour and removed the crown from my head. He tears me down on every side till I am gone; he uproots my hope like a tree" (Job 19:8-10).

Jeremiah, who was known as the weeping prophet, was called to prophesy. His job was to call the stubborn and rebellious children of Israel to repentance and to return to the covenant they had made with God. He was beaten and imprisoned, and at one point he was even thrown down a well – such was the appreciation he received for his services! Paul suffered so much at one point that he said:

"We do not want you to be uninformed, brothers and sisters, about the troubles we experienced in the province of Asia. We were under great pressure, far beyond our ability to endure, so that we despaired of life itself. Indeed, we felt we had received the sentence of death. But this happened that we might not rely on ourselves but on God, who raises the dead" (2 Corinthians 1:8-9).

During our lives there will be seasons of great joy, but there will also be dark and difficult days. During those days, we are encouraged by Isaiah to remain confident in God, to draw close to Him and to really trust and lean upon Him:

"Who is among you who [reverently] fears the Lord, who obeys the voice of His Servant, yet who walks in darkness *and* deep trouble and has no shining splendor [in his heart]? Let him rely on, trust in, *and* be confident in the name of the Lord, and let him lean upon *and* be supported by his God" (Isaiah 50:10, AMP).

I can honestly say that God kept and sustained us through our challenging season. He brought the right people alongside us at the right moments, and they prayed, supported and encouraged us. Throughout that season He provided all that we needed financially in all kinds of ways and means. He kept us going. He brought peace, joy and hope. He strengthened us when we felt weak and kept us going when we wanted to crawl under a stone and quit.

God has a plan

He also gently reminded me that He had a plan:

"'For I know the plans I have for you,' declares the Lord, 'plans to prosper you and not to harm you, plans to give you hope and a future'" (Jeremiah 29:11).

This verse is well known and often quoted (sometimes out of context); however, God used it to speak profoundly to me. It's a wonderful promise, but the main thing God said to me was this: "I have a plan." I remember being so encouraged by this. I wasn't particularly taken by the promise of prosperity or hope or a future, but quite simply that God had a plan. I couldn't see it, but God had one – and that was enough for me!

God knows your situation. It hasn't taken Him by surprise at all. He knew it was going to happen, and He has a plan. As you read this, be assured that God is ready to help and prepared to step in, and He is already working everything together for your good.

He has made those plans for us, and He knows them intimately, but until He reveals them our job is to be patient; to pray and wait and trust. That's tough sometimes. It's a place of surrender to the One who knows best. Sometimes we can be tempted to make things happen ourselves, but it's far better to wait for God to bring about a change to our circumstances or open the right doors.

God also said to me very clearly: '*I* know the plan and *you* don't!' I remember thinking to myself, *Well that's great, but is there any possibility you could let me in on this secret?*

Of course, God has a plan in every season of our lives, but I would add that He also has a purpose. The plan details what will happen over the years, while the purpose explains the objective of this plan. For example, His plan may be for us to be part of a local church, while His purpose may be for us to feel connected to others and to Him as a result, and to mature in our faith and bring Him glory through our membership. He never wastes any opportunity to fulfil His purposes in our lives and in the lives of those around us. Whatever you are facing right now, please be encouraged that God has a plan and a purpose. This season you are going through will not be in vain, it will not be wasted. It is all part of God's overall plan and purpose.

Praying, waiting and trusting

As I was seeking God one morning during this season, I found myself praying:

Father, help me to pray, to wait and to trust.
Help me to wait and trust after I've prayed.
Help me to trust and pray while I wait.
Help me to trust while I wait and pray.

I realised that the three were, in fact, interchangeable. They work together well, and there is a powerful synergy when we do all three.

So, PRAY, WAIT, TRUST.

My desire for this book is to share with you some of the principles I learned during this season of praying, waiting and trusting, in the hope that it will encourage and empower you to keep going – confident in the knowledge that God has a plan and a purpose, and will bring you through. You may even wish to make the prayer above your own prayer as we commence this journey together.

Part One

"Don't worry about anything; instead, pray about everything. Tell God what you need, and thank him for all he has done. Then you will experience God's peace, which exceeds anything we can understand. His peace will guard your hearts and minds as you live in Christ Jesus." (Philippians 4:6-7, NLT)

Chapter One

Pray

I have seen some incredible answers to prayer over the years. In my personal and family life I've witnessed God's incredible provision, breakthroughs and healings. I've seen Him completely turn situations around, change people, open previously closed doors and make the seemingly impossible become possible. In addition, He has often granted me the desires of my heart as I have sought, as best I can, to delight myself in Him (see Psalm 37:5).

However, having been thrown the curveball I mentioned in the Introduction, I found praying during our wilderness season really challenging. Don't forget that I'm a pastor, so praying is what I do! Yet I discovered there are only so many ways, after all, that you can pray the same thing – in my case: "I need a job." For you it might be: "I need a home, I need healing, I need cash, I need a relationship to change, I need a breakthrough..."

What do you pray after you have prayed everything you can think of? What do you pray when you've prayed in every way you can and renounced all your sins (several times!), but there still appears to be no change in your circumstances?

While we're in the praying, waiting and trusting zone, prayer can become almost mechanical if we're not careful; something that is performed out of duty. When times are tough, when the days seem to last forever and nothing seems to change, praying can become really hard... and waiting on God (never mind hearing his voice!) is harder still. I quickly found myself becoming restless and bored with praying the same prayers, with believing in God, with expecting Him to intervene despite nothing changing.

I can understand why the disciples said to Jesus: "Lord, teach us to pray!"

Here are some of the things I learned about prayer during the toughest of seasons.

The Lord's Prayer

One of my greatest rediscoveries was the Lord's Prayer. I cannot adequately express the impact this had on my life during the season of waiting, when I really struggled to pray or to know what to actually say when I prayed.

I've added it below. Can I encourage you to read it slowly, out loud? Repeat each line and allow the Holy Spirit to lead you into other prayers, places and thoughts as you take your time to speak out the words of the prayer Jesus taught His disciples to pray.

Our Father, who art in heaven,
hallowed be thy name;
Thy kingdom come;
Thy will be done;
on earth as it is in heaven.
Give us this day our daily bread

And forgive us our trespasses,
as we forgive those who trespass against us.
And lead us not into temptation;
but deliver us from evil.
For thine is the kingdom,
the power and the glory,
for ever and ever.
Amen.[1]

There is something really powerful about the Lord's Prayer that many of us haven't tapped into yet. It is a prayer for every season of life, but it has been of particular value to me in really challenging seasons. At those times it becomes a foundational prayer; a prayer to base our praying on. A prayer that sets the scene and our perspective in the right place: on Father God.

My praying hit a whole new level as I prayed this powerful prayer. The Bible informs us that God inhabits the praises of His people (see Psalm 22:3). I would add that God, the Holy Spirit, inhabits His Word. I felt the presence of the Saviour numerous times as I prayed His words out loud. The very presence of the Jesus who spoke these words for the first time some 2,000 years ago continued to inhabit the prayer He had taught His disciples to pray.

The psalms

I was already aware of how inspiring and life-giving the psalms were, but as we navigated through our long waiting season, they became a daily blessing. It felt as if there was one for almost every situation and circumstance of our lives. For example, in a period of his life when he felt as if God had forsaken him, David cried out in this wonderful messianic psalm:

"God, my God! Why would you abandon me now? Why do you remain distant, refusing to answer my tearful cries in the day and my desperate cries for your help in the night? I can't stop sobbing. Where are you, my God?" (Psalms 22:1-2, TPT).

And later:

"But I am a worm and not a man, scorned by everyone, despised by the people. All who see me mock me; they hurl insults, shaking their heads. 'He trusts in the Lord,' they say, 'let the Lord rescue him. Let him deliver him, since he delights in him'" (Psalms 22:6-8).

The psalms are written with honesty, vulnerability and transparency, and I've found that they not only help me verbalise how I'm feeling, but they also help me to refocus on God and refresh my perspective. They deliver truth, renew hope, restore strength and encourage me to persevere, not to quit. They are so good!

As you pray, wait and trust, how about working your way through the psalms? Try taking one each day. Read it, meditate on it, pray those God-breathed words out loud and use those age-old truths as a foundation for your own prayers. Allow God to speak and minister deeply to you through them.

---

1. 'The Lord's Prayer (Traditional version), The Church of England: (accessed 14 August 2023).

Chapter Two

What is prayer?

We all know how important prayer is, and perhaps it is even more important when we're going through a challenging season. If we're honest, none of us (pastors included!) pray enough, and when times are good we probably pray less than when they are difficult. We know that prayer is something we should do, but what exactly is it?

Prayer is a place of acceptance, belonging and healing

"Let us then approach God's throne of grace with confidence, so that we may receive mercy and find grace to help us in our time of need" (Hebrews 4:16).

As we come before the Father, we receive acceptance and forgiveness. It's a place of love, mercy and grace. He does not treat us as our sins deserve, but rather He loves us with an everlasting love. I've discovered that even when I've wilfully done wrong, even when I find myself in a waiting and trusting season because of my own mistakes and choices, His grace and mercy overflows. He has more than enough to cover me.

It may be that other people have discarded and discounted you. They may have rejected you, unfairly judged you, treated you appallingly and caused you unfathomable anguish, hurt and pain. They may well be the reason for the season you are in right now. That's really hard for any of us to accept.

However, no matter what anyone else thinks or says, you are God's precious son or daughter. You are the apple of His eye. You are loved and accepted. You belong in His family, and are always welcome in His presence when you seek Him in prayer. Know this in your heart and let no one convince you otherwise.

He is also your healer. If the past season has caused you hurt, pain or anguish, let me encourage you to reach out to Him. Ask Him to forgive those who have sinned against you, and to heal all your wounds. You may need help with this. If so, why not reach out to a friend you trust or your pastor, and ask them to pray with you?

Prayer is a place of fellowship and communion with the Holy Spirit

The Greek word for "fellowship", *koinonia*, suggests a deep sense of communion with God and with others.[1] This is a level of intimacy that is not found in simple friendships. Paul reminds us:

"May the grace of the Lord Jesus Christ, and the love of God, and the fellowship of the Holy Spirit be with you all" (2 Corinthians 13:14).

Many of us have experienced the grace of Jesus Christ and the incredible love of God, but we so often neglect the precious fellowship of the Holy Spirit. There is something wonderful about simply sitting in the presence of God and enjoying sweet fellowship with Him.

"Be still before the Lord and wait patiently for him" (Psalm 37:7).

During the waiting season I continued, as is my habit, to rise early each morning, sit in my chair, pray and still myself before God as I waited on Him. In those moments of stillness and prayer, I experienced deeply the gentleness and quietness of His presence.

As Isaiah put it:

"For thus said the Lord God, the Holy One of Israel: In returning [to Me] and resting [in Me] you shall be saved; in quietness and in [trusting] confidence shall be your strength." (Isaiah 30:15, AMP).

I wonder if God is using this season you are going through to draw you back to Him, inviting you to trust in Him once again. Perhaps you and God have become a little distant. Perhaps you need to rediscover the power of being still in His presence. If we will be like Mary, rather than Martha, and stop rushing around in all the crazy busyness of our lives, and take some time to draw near to God, we will discover that His presence in our lives will help and sustain us during the toughest of seasons.

As Duncan Clark wrote: "We really must learn how to sit quietly and enjoy fellowship with the Holy Spirit."[2]

As we learn to slow down and sit quietly in His presence, we will discover that God is able to satisfy and fulfil our deepest needs. We can just sit quietly, enjoying Him, meditating on His Word or lost in worship. However, His promise to us is clear:

"Draw near to God and he will draw near to you" (James 4:8, NKJV).

Prayer is the place where we can draw near to God, where He promises to draw near to us. Time spent in His presence enables us to have deep communion with God. The true meaning of "communion" is "sharing".[3] When we have fellowship with the Holy Spirit, we are sharing our lives with God, and He with us.

This is what Adam and Eve experienced in the Garden of Eden before the fall. Every day, God would come and walk with them in the garden. Tragically, they were ejected from the garden because of their sin. But thankfully, through Jesus' death and resurrection, that sweet and nourishing fellowship is once again available to all who put their trust in Him.

This is the fellowship and deep communion God longs to have with us as individuals. It is our very lifeblood. The tragedy is that, for all kinds of reasons – and in particular because we lead such busy lives – we often miss out on this vital, life-affirming and life-giving source. Of course, as I have discovered for myself, this type of communion is even more important during a season of waiting and trusting in God.

Jesus himself said:

"'I am the vine; you are the branches. If you remain in me and I in you, you will bear much fruit; apart from me you can do nothing'" (John 15:5).

Let me encourage you during this season to prioritise your time with God. Enjoy fellowship with the Holy Spirit. Commune with Him. Dwell. Walk. Talk. Share. Remain. Be.

As you do this, you will sense His peace in ways that go beyond your own understanding. You will experience His joy inconceivable, His love overflowing. Your hope will arise and your faith will increase as He draws close. God is everything we need, and without Him we have nothing. During this season, pursue a relationship with Him.

Carey Nieuwhof sums it up well: "Prayer is not a button to be pushed. It's a relationship to be pursued."[4]

This current season is an opportunity to deepen your relationship with the Father, to get to know Him better and to learn to depend on Him more. As I look back over my life, I realise that every challenging season has deepened my relationship with my Father, strengthened my faith and increased my dependency on Him. I would not have wanted to miss what I gained during those times. These experiences have been foundational in my life and faith.

Prayer is surrender to the One who knows best

The Lord's Prayer teaches us to pray, "Thy kingdom come; thy will be done", and that suggests to me that whenever we pray we are expected to surrender our lives and our needs to God. In fact, every time we pray, we're recognising our need of God's hand on our lives and His help in navigating the day-to-day. We're recognising our need to surrender to the One who knows best.

The waiting seasons force us to depend totally on Him. This is an important life lesson that God, in His wisdom, wants us to learn. He is the One we must learn to depend on. He is totally trustworthy. He will never let us down. Apart from Him we can do nothing (as we read in John 15:5). Learn to abide in the true vine.

Prayer also means surrendering to God's timing rather than doing things our own way. A day is like a thousand years and a thousand years is like a day to Him. Sometimes we have to wait for a period of time before we receive an answer to our prayers. God is never, ever in the hurry we are – frustrating as that might be!

He uses that time to do some work in us. He hones and refines, and He builds faith, patience, character and trust. He will never miss the opportunity to use these seasons for our good because He wants to put strong foundations into our lives. As Craig Groeschel says:

"Sometimes God may want to do something IN you before He does something FOR you."[5]

If you haven't already, let me encourage you to surrender your life again to the One who knows best. He really does know best. I've found there is something incredibly releasing in surrendering our lives to God. I don't believe He ever anticipated that our lives would be a one-time-only surrender to Him on the day we became Christians. Rather, it is a daily response to His leading in our lives.

When was the last time you took a moment to surrender every aspect of your life to Him? You will be better for it, and it may be that God is simply waiting for your surrender before He begins to release the bottleneck and move things forward for you.

Why don't you pause before going any further and surrender your life afresh to Him? Go through each area of your life as you pray, and invite Him to become Lord of lords and King of kings once again.

Prayer creates the opportunity for a divine exchange

Martin Luther said: "Pray, and let God worry."[6]

This is great advice! Don't worry – pray! Prayer helps us to stop worrying. You cannot worry and pray at the same time. You will discover as you pour out your heart to Him that a divine exchange takes place. You exchange doubts, fears, stress, uncertainty and worries for the peace of God that passes all understanding and the wonderful joy of the Lord. As a bonus you will experience the love of God, and a renewed faith and hope in Him.

"'Come to me, all you who are weary and burdened, and I will give you rest. Take my yoke upon you and learn from me, for I am gentle and humble in heart, and you will find rest for your souls. For my yoke is easy and my burden is light'" (Matthew 11:28-30).

I remember hearing those words for the first time as a boy, sitting in a marquee as evening prayers took place at the camp I was attending in beautiful North Wales. These powerful words of Jesus were sung by us in a simple chorus, and I'm sure there are people all over the world today who remember and draw on them during times when they are praying, waiting and trusting God.

The heart of the Father is to allow us to unburden ourselves on Him. He never created us to be weary and burdened, but rather to take His divine yoke, which is intended to be light and easy. God eternally purposed each of us to be involved in creating, building and managing His kingdom on earth alongside the busyness of homes, families and work. There will of course be curveballs and times of challenge, seasons of change and paths to navigate, but through it all we must stick close to Him and learn how to carry our responsibilities lightly. It can be done. It is a learned practice.

Perhaps as you are reading this you find yourself burdened with anxieties and cares. Perhaps you have taken on burdens that God never asked you to carry. If so, let me encourage you to take a moment (right now if possible) to unburden yourself before Him. Let go of those burdens and enter His rest. Then only pick up the specific burdens He has asked you to carry.

"Cast all your anxiety on him because he cares for you" (1 Peter 5:7).

David writes:

"Cast your cares on the Lord and he will sustain you; he will never let the righteous be shaken" (Psalms 55:22).

May God help each of us to learn the secret of letting go and allowing God to carry and sustain us throughout our lives, as He has promised:

"Even to your old age and grey hairs I am he, I am he who will sustain you. I have made you and I will carry you; I will sustain you and I will rescue you" (Isaiah 46:4).

Don't panic!

One of my favourite comedy series when I was growing up was *Dad's Army*. It was about a lacklustre platoon of men who joined the Home Guard during the Second World War. Their objective was to protect Britain should Hitler attempt an invasion, and they were led by the pompous and completely incompetent Captain Mainwaring. One of the other main characters was called Corporal Jones, whose catchphrase was: 'Don't panic! Don't panic!' The irony was that he would shout this every time he and those around him were panicking!

Prayer removes panic. Perhaps you're beginning to panic right now about the way your life is headed and you're wondering what will happen. *Where is God? Will He come through for me? Why have my prayers still not been answered?* Allow your prayers to replace and remove your panic. Learn to rest in Him:

"Let be and be still, and know (recognise and understand) that I am God" (Psalm 46:10, AMP).

This verse encourages us to pause in the middle of our circumstances and acknowledge before God where we are at, and then to be still and freshly grasp that He is God. What has happened did not come as a surprise to God. He is still sovereign and in control. Allow God to replace your panic with His peace.

Prayer creates the perfect opportunity for God to speak

During challenging seasons it can be hard enough to pray, never mind hear God's voice. But if we persevere in spending time communing with Him, we will discover that He has things to say that will bring comfort, hope, peace, joy, encouragement and insight, and will provide the strength we need to keep going.

After nine months of having no job or regular income, I felt God say to me, "Look wider than your denomination." To be honest I was a little horrified, as the Elim Pentecostal Church had been our family for some thirty years. We had so many wonderful friends and colleagues. How could we ever consider leaving and pastoring an independent church?

Anyhow, I eventually applied for the role in Banbury. Lots of confirmations followed, and we very much felt called to help rebuild this church post-pandemic. Nearly two years on, we are very much enjoying leading this lovely, growing church family, and we have fully remained part of the Elim family. In fact, as I write, our church has just been accepted into the Elim network. God is good. God knows best. We need to listen to His voice.

Perhaps during your waiting season, God is waiting to speak.

God speaks in so many ways

There have been many times when I have lacked clarity and haven't known what to do, and God has spoken to me with words of wisdom, comfort, peace, guidance and direction... words I would never have received had I not been open and willing to listen to His voice.

In my experience, God speaks in a variety of ways, but primarily through His Word – the Bible. His Word is living and active, and sharper than any two-edged sword (see Hebrews 4:12). God will use it to speak into your situation. Try to read His Word every day, and give Him the opportunity to speak to you through it.

"Whether you turn to the right or to the left, your ears will hear a voice behind you, saying, 'This is the way; walk in it'" (Isaiah 30:21).

Attune your ears to Him

There have been many occasions over the years when God has spoken while I've been praying. Sometimes it happened while I was sitting with a mug of coffee in a comfy chair in a quiet spot. Other times it happened as I walked through the beautiful local countryside.

I've discovered that as I attune my ears to Him, He plants thoughts, impressions, pictures, scriptures, desires and leadings into my heart in order to communicate His will. I believe He also whispers into our ears at times when we aren't even praying. This has happened on so many occasions. I can be driving, showering, running or doing anything other than actually praying, and He gently whispers something into my ear.

This is something that has developed for me over the years as I have cultivated my relationship with my Father. Those leanings, thoughts, impressions and whispers are sometimes easy for the untrained ear to discard. Have you missed anything from God lately? Seriously, this is worth considering. If so, ask Him to remind you.

God will use the still, small voice within you and heavenly whispers to speak to you. He is the good, good Father and He loves to speak to His children. What good parent doesn't? So be led by His Spirit as you pray. He may ask you to do something specific: to confess sin, be obedient in some area of your life, do something symbolic or pray in a certain place or with a particular person.

Be open to His leading, and always test what you hear against His Word. Never make any life-changing decisions without fully praying them through, listening to wise counsel and seeking numerous confirmations.

God will speak through others

While Julia and I were considering our move to the church in Banbury, friends repeatedly shared that they had been praying for us and had seen a picture of a jigsaw. As they looked closely, they saw that it had one missing piece. And when the missing piece was revealed, they saw our faces on it. We were, in fact, the missing piece! On the day of our final discussions, when we were dotting the "i"s and crossing the "t"s, one of the elders shared exactly the same picture. We knew we had heard from God.

Perhaps God will use this waiting season to enable you to hear His voice more clearly. When life was good you probably didn't need to depend on Him or hear His voice as much. Maybe God is using this opportunity to train your spiritual ears in order to equip you for all that He has planned for you in the future. As God's people, we all need to be alert and ready to hear His voice.

"Lead me in the right path, O Lord, or my enemies will conquer me. Make your way plain for me to follow" (Psalm 5:8, NLT).

Prayer opens the storehouses of heaven

"Prayer is the key that unlocks all the storehouses of God's infinite grace and power. All that God is, and all that God has, is at the disposal of prayer" (R. A. Torrey).[7]

I mentioned earlier that I have seen God answer prayer many times. He has an incredible track record. One of the best examples of this relates to my eldest daughter's wedding. We so wanted to give Sarah the day of her dreams, but had little money to spare. Pastors aren't the highest-paid people in the land and weddings are expensive. Why is it that everything needed for a wedding is twice the price compared with any other event? Anyway, we prayed.

God provided a lovely cricket club for the venue that was big enough for all the guests Sarah and Martin wanted to invite; Christian caterers who provided great food at a ridiculously low cost; a photographer friend who took the photos for free; another friend who made Sarah's stunning wedding dress and a friend's daughter who provided the cake. Another friend gifted us a substantial amount of money that covered pretty much everything else and, to cap it all, it was a beautifully warm autumn day in Newcastle. We prayed about every single resource we needed for the wedding and God opened all the storehouses of His provision. Amazing! We had a truly wonderful day.

Prayer opens heaven's storehouses. However, God can't answer prayers you are not praying. So pray! The God who provided for you in the past is the same loving Father today. He is not a reluctant Father; He is more than willing to meet every need you may have.

Prayer brings strength

The waiting season can be lonely, wearying and desperate at times. Julia and I both found it really hard. Then one morning I came across this verse:

"But the Lord stood at my side and gave me strength" (2 Timothy 4:17).

I cannot express how encouraged I was as I read those words. Often it takes time for our circumstances to change, but this was an encouraging reminder that the Lord was with me, standing right by my side and giving me the strength to face each new day. I cannot emphasise how revitalised I felt as I read that verse. I stood on that promise for days, and every time I prayed and meditated on it I felt like I was being infused with fresh energy, power and strength.

Prayer builds us up. The season of waiting can be incredibly long and arduous at times, and we need His strength to come through it.

"But those who trust in the Lord will find new strength. They will soar high on wings like eagles. They will run and not grow weary. They will walk and not faint" (Isaiah 40:31, NLT).

The promise is this: there is renewed strength every day as we trust in Him.

---

1. J. Brodie, 'What Every Christian Needs to Know about Koinonia', Crosswalk, 25 April 2022: (accessed 14 August 2023).

2. D. Clark, Twitter, 28 July 2023: https://twitter.com/pastordunc (accessed 14 August 2023).

3. J. Brodie, 'What Every Christian Needs to Know about Koinonia', Crosswalk, 25 April 2022: (accessed 14 August 2023).

4. C. Nieuwhof, Twitter, 22 March 2021: (accessed 14 August 2023).

5. C. Groeschel, Instagram, 19 July 2023: (accessed 14 August 2023).

6. Mcdanell99, 'Pray And Let God Worry: The Context', Sola Evangeli, 16 October 2014: (accessed 14 August 2023).

7. R. A. Torrey, The Power of Prayer, Kindle edition (New Kensington, PA: Whitaker House, 2000), p. 195.

Chapter Three

How to pray when you don't know what to pray

I n the same way the Spirit [comes to us and] helps us in our
weakness. We do not know what prayer to offer or how to offer it
as we should, but the Spirit Himself [knows our need and at the right
time] intercedes on our behalf with sighs *and* groanings too deep
for words. And He who searches the hearts knows what the mind
of the Spirit is, because the Spirit intercedes [before God] on behalf
of God's people in accordance with God's will. (Romans 8:26-27,
AMP)

I believe the Holy Spirit works through our silence, and through
our inner groans, longings and cries, during those long waiting seasons. In those times when we cry out in desperation with no words,
in our ignorance of what to pray or do, the Holy Spirit is interceding
with the Father on our behalf.

Twice Paul mentions that, at these very moments, the Holy Spirit takes our suffering, longings and desires, and represents us before the Father with sighs and groans too deep for words. There is no suggestion in Paul's writing of what the Spirit actually says, but my guess is that He communicates the depth of our sufferings, longings and desires to God, and that He intercedes before the Father on our behalf, in accordance with God's will. Wow! What a thought.

The postscript to the verse above is this:

"And we know [with great confidence] that God [who is deeply concerned about us] causes all things to work together [as a plan] for good for those who love God, to those who are called according to His plan *and* purpose" (Romans 8:28, AMP).

You may not have been the greatest prayer in the past, and you may well be wondering, *How on earth do I actually pray?* Charles Spurgeon has some great advice:

"Still prayer itself is an art which only the Holy Ghost can teach us. He is the giver of all prayer. Pray for prayer – pray till you can pray; pray to be helped to pray, and give not up praying because thou canst not pray, for it is when thou thinkest thou canst not pray that thou art most praying; and sometimes when thou hast no sort of comfort in thy supplications, it is then that thy heart all broken and cast down is really wrestling and truly prevailing with the Most High."[1]

As does Samuel Chadwick:

"There is no way to learn to pray but by praying. No reasoned philosophy of prayer ever taught a soul to pray. The subject is beset with problems, but there are no problems of prayer to the man who prays. They are all met in the fact of answered prayer and the joy of fellowship with God."[2]

The more time you spend in prayer, talking to God, the more you will discover a pattern that works for you. We all connect with God differently in prayer. It's a journey, so don't be too hard on yourself. Take it day by day as you develop and cultivate your relationship with God.

I've put together ten practical suggestions to help you.

1. Make prayer a habit

It seems clear to me that prayer and fellowship with God become even more critical during the seasons of waiting and trusting Him. We must remember that, while God will use these seasons to increase our faith and build resilience in us, our enemy – the devil – will see this as an opportunity to pick us off. His sole aim is to steal, kill and destroy your faith (see John 10:10). Don't allow him to do so. Stay close to God. Pray more. Pray every day. Plan your prayer times. Put them in your diary and use technology to remind you.

One pattern that has helped me is this: I rise early to spend time with God. This is the first thing I do every day – apart from putting the kettle on for a nice cup of Yorkshire tea (other brands are available!). During this time I will worship, read God's Word, wait on Him and pray through a long prayer list that includes family, friends, church, community, the world, etc.).

Be careful that you don't get stuck in a rut in your times with God. Vary it. Worship, read a devotional book, go for a walk and pray. Play soaking music while you pray or sit in silence. Meditate on a particular verse. Invest in your relationship with God. Read books about prayer. Glean from the saints of old what worked for them. Be creative and keep it fresh.

During the day I use a shorter list containing the more important prayer needs from the main list. This is on my Microsoft To Do app list, and at various points during the day (normally at least twice) I will look at this list and stop what I'm doing to work through it. I will ask, seek and knock on heaven's door for breakthroughs and provision for others, for my church and for my family. This has proven highly effective. Over the years I have seen God answer so many of these prayers.

On other occasions I will sit (preferably with a mug of tea) and just engage in what I call freestyle prayer, where I just worship and talk to God about whatever is on *my* heart and allow Him to gently lead me to pray the things that are on *His* heart. No rush, no lists, no pressure. Just my Father and me having some time together.

It's also a good idea to pray with your spouse or a friend, if you can. Julia and I have seen some incredible breakthroughs and answers to prayer as a result. Didn't Jesus say something about this?

"'I also tell you this: If two of you agree here on earth concerning anything you ask, my Father in heaven will do it for you'" (Matthew 18:19, NLT).

2. Step it up!

I've discovered there are seasons in our lives when we need to step up our praying and really seek God.

"As for me, I call to God, and the Lord saves me. Evening, morning and noon I cry out in distress, and he hears my voice" (Psalms 55:16-17).

Wasn't it James who challenged the early believers about the inadequacy of their prayer lives?

"You do not have because you do not ask God" (James 4:2).

Here's the thing: if you want to see change, If you want to see God break through, if you want to see the impossible become possible, the doors open and the miraculous happen, you must pray more! You may need to fast, too. No bones about it – you will need to step it up.

3. Start your prayer with thanksgiving and worship

"Do not be anxious about anything, but in every situation, by prayer and petition, with thanksgiving, present your requests to God" (Philippians 4:6).

It's so easy to be negative. We live in a world where we're surrounded by negativity, criticism and judgement. I recently had to remind myself to focus on the positives rather than the negatives, and to be thankful. As soon as I did, I began to realise things weren't anywhere near as bad as they appeared. In fact, they were pretty good.

When you start looking, you can find things every day to be thankful for, and you can even enjoy moments of joy and laughter. This is important during a tough season when it's difficult to know what to do or how to pray. So make sure that you build thanksgiving and worship into your life. Don't wait for Sunday!

4. Worship

One of the things I discovered as I began to use the Lord's Prayer in my praying was the value of worship. I would start my prayers by quietening by heart and slowly praying His prayer. I would routinely get 'stuck' at the point of 'hallowed be thy name', which caused me to pause and simply worship with a grateful heart. I remembered the absolute privilege of being able to worship, abide and talk to my God. It focused my attention on Him, not on me or my needs. I found it centred me in the right place as I sat in His presence. It raised my faith levels, removed my unbelief and enabled me to expect and believe for more than I could possibly ask or imagine:

"Never doubt God's mighty power to work in you and accomplish all this. He will achieve infinitely more than your greatest request, your most unbelievable dream, and exceed your wildest imagination! He will outdo them all, for his miraculous power constantly energizes you" (Ephesians 3:20, TPT.)

This is such a great way to start praying... and continue praying!

How many of us just dash in with a list of needs? How many of us are tempted to focus solely on what we don't have right now? It's much better to focus on all that God has. Heaven's storeroom is always full. There is no lack there. He can meet our every need.

I cannot emphasise enough how important worship is. In the midst of difficult times, we simply *must* keep our focus on Him. The devil would love to drag us into a place of despondency and despair, but we must somehow stay in a place of faith, expectation and belief that better days lie ahead.

Worship changes the spiritual atmosphere around us and brings us into God's presence. Worship restores perspective, releases tension, lifts our heads, builds us up, restores courage, edifies our spirits, encourages our hearts and strengthens our resolve to keep going. Worship allows us to forget about ourselves and our situations; to lose ourselves in His presence. It's wonderful!

5. Stand on His Word and His promises

"The Lord is faithful to all His promises and loving towards all He has made" (Psalm 145:13).

Our prayers are strengthened and pack more power when we stand on God's Word. After all, He has declared that His Word will not return empty to Him and will achieve the purpose for which it was sent (see Isaiah 55:11).

I've discovered the power of standing on His Word and declaring His truth and promises over my life, my family, my friends and His Church. There is a powerful synergy that occurs when we stand on His Word.

As Spurgeon put it:

"After all, prayer is nothing but taking God's promises to him, and saying to him, 'Do as thou hast said.' Prayer is the promise utilized. A prayer which is not based on a promise has no true foundation. If I go to the bank without a cheque I need not expect to get money; it is the 'order to pay' which is my power inside the bank, and my warrant for expecting to receive."[3]

I've learned to stand on His promises in particular situations and when I have particular needs, and I've seen breakthrough after breakthrough over the years. It may take time, but God always comes through. He is faithful to all His promises. All his promises are "yes" and "amen" (see 2 Corinthians 1:20).

I've also discovered that His promises are a source of strength and encouragement. I'm so thankful for them.

As the psalmist declares:

"I hang on to these words for dear life! These words hold me up in bad times; yes, your promises rejuvenate me" (Psalms 119:50, MSG).

6. Use the prayers He gives you

The more you pray, the more you will learn to pray. A recent development for me has been my discovery that the Holy Spirit will sometimes lead and guide me into the most powerful prayers, which carry unusual weight and authority. I've begun to recognise this as the Holy Spirit praying through me. I would humbly suggest that what I sense at these moments is that I am praying in God's will.

The Bible makes it clear that when we pray according to the Father's will, it will be done for us:

"This is the confidence we have in approaching God: that if we ask anything according to his will, he hears us. And if we know that he hears us – whatever we ask – we know that we have what we asked of him" (1 John 5:14-15).

Wow! What confidence we have before God as we are led to pray these Spirit-led, power-packed prayers. When this occurs, I've become aware that I need to add these prayers to my list and pray every day – several times a day – until it happens. I could share many examples of this. On one occasion I was praying, and a few days earlier I'd been reading the book of Nehemiah, and so I found myself praying very similar words to those in his prayers: "Remember me, O my God", "Remember me with favour" (see Nehemiah 5:19, 13:14, 22, 31). Over a period of time, as I prayed this simple prayer over my personal circumstances and our church, I saw God move wonderfully in opening doors and using others (who remembered me!) to provide some of the things we needed. He certainly remembered me during that season.

Often it will just be a simple sentence or paragraph, and I can honestly say that, almost without exception, these prayers have been answered. Why? Because they are Holy Spirit-inspired prayers, their source is heaven, and they are prayed in the Father's will.

"Your kingdom come, your will be done, on earth as it is in heaven" (Matthew 6:10).

Perhaps, like me, your ongoing prayer should be this: "Lord, continue to teach me to pray."

7. Ask, seek, knock

Towards the end of my mother's life, I regularly drove from Banbury to her home in Leicester to visit her. Sadly, she retreated into a bit of a shell in the last few months and didn't really want to see anybody. The first time this occurred, I knocked, rang the doorbell and called her phone several times. Eventually, I got an answer, the door opened and I was given access to the house. I had to be persistent.

I could have given up, but then the journey would have been a waste of time. I almost drove away; I came really close to it. I almost missed the opportunity to see my mother open the door because I didn't feel like persisting any longer. It turned out she had been resting in a bedroom at the back of the house and apparently hadn't heard me.

Jesus taught the disciples to pray, and he said:

"'Ask and it will be given to you; seek and you will find; knock and the door will be opened to you. For everyone who asks receives; the one who seeks finds; and to the one who knocks, the door will be opened" (Matthew 7:7-8).

Ask
Seek
Knock

It's interesting that Jesus encouraged us to do all three. He wanted us to pray without ceasing. He wanted us to ask, that we would receive; to seek, that we would find; to knock, that the door would be opened. Just like trying to attract my mum's attention, prayer requires persistence at times.

Jesus told the parable of the persistent widow to demonstrate this. Luke introduces the parable as follows: "Then Jesus told his disciples a parable to show them that they should always pray and not give up" (Luke 18:1).

The persistent widow eventually received justice because she cried out for it day and night. Sadly, I rarely hear of a Christian praying in this way or with such faith. When explaining the parable, Jesus hinted that persisting and pleading in prayer is not simply a sign of

30

desperation; it is actually a sign of someone with great faith! This person knows that God will answer, so he or she keeps on praying!

When we're waiting for a long time for God to break through, change a situation or open a door, it can become incredibly discouraging... and sadly that's when we may be tempted to stop praying.

"What's the point?" the enemy will whisper in your ear. "Why bother? Nothing's changing. Nothing will ever change! Why waste your time?"

So... ignore him! Don't quit. Keep praying.

Just recently I went to fill up my car with petrol. As I drove onto the garage forecourt, all the pumps were in use and there were queues behind each one. Frustrated and impatient, I pulled away from the queue I was in and drove home because I was unwilling to wait for an available pump. The next day I returned and the price had gone up! Not one of my better calls.

None of us like waiting. We want it *now*! We cannot wait. We *refuse* to wait. It's little wonder that we struggle to pray consistently and persistently.

"Rejoice always *and* delight in your faith; be unceasing *and* persistent in prayer; in every situation [no matter what the circumstances] be thankful *and* continually give thanks *to God*; for this is the will of God for you in Christ Jesus" (1 Thessalonians 5:16-18, AMP).

Here's the thing: when we fail to pray continually and persistently, we miss out on a faith-building exercise and the sheer joy of receiving the answer. Have you ever prayed about something for weeks, months or even years and suddenly it comes to pass? What joy! What fulfilment! What spiritual growth! What faith for the future!

Let me encourage you in this waiting season to trust God and to keep persisting in prayer. Don't quit during the gap between the prayer and the provision.

8. Set time aside to wait on God

Prayer must be a two-way conversation; however, hearing God's voice can be a challenge during a tough season. Our motivation may be poor, our faith small and our feelings all over the place. If we have been waiting for God to answer for a long time, we can easily become disenchanted to the point where we question the value of prayer. You may even have found yourself asking God, "Why can't you just *sort this out*?!"

In the midst of the frustration, pressures, disappointment and discouragement, it can be even harder to sit down and quiet your heart to the point where you are able to hear God's voice. I mentioned earlier that prayer creates an opportunity for God to speak, and that in my experience He will also begin to speak to us at times when we aren't actually praying.

Having said this, it is really important to set time aside to pray and seek His face. Jeremiah reminds us that when we seek Him we will find him and be found by Him (see Jeremiah 29:13-14). God also declared through the prophet:

"'Call to me and I will answer you and tell you great and unsearchable things you do not know'" (Jeremiah 33:3).

What if God wants to speak to you? What if He wants to reveal something to you that you don't yet know? What if He wants to bring fresh direction to the season you're in? What if He has a solution?

What if He simply wants to encourage you while you wait? What if He wants to remind you of something He's already said?

Can I encourage you to purposefully set some time aside to do this? Initially, I would suggest you just set aside 30-60 minutes perhaps once a week or month. You'll need to find a quiet space (preferably an empty home or office with a comfortable chair) where you won't be disturbed. Switch all your devices to 'do not disturb' (most devices can be set to allow emergency calls from close family) and let significant people know you don't want to be disturbed during this time (I find this releases me to focus).

Then quieten your heart before God by confessing any known sin and bringing any anxious thoughts or concerns before Him, releasing you to focus entirely on Him. Take a few deep breaths and become aware of His presence around you. I find worship also really helps and particularly 'soaking music', which is available on most music apps. Anointed Christian instrumental music is a great aid to entering God's presence and hearing His voice. In 2 Kings 3:15, Elisha called for a harpist so he could hear God's voice and bring prophetic insight for King Jehoshaphat, the king of Israel and the king of Edom in their battle with the Moabites. As a result, a great victory was won (2 Kings 3:24-27).

Be led by God as you wait, but at some point you may wish to turn the music off and just wait in silence. Make sure you're comfortable and that you posture yourself in expectation of God speaking. I sometimes find it helpful to simply repeat the name of "Jesus" or "I love you, Lord" or "Father", which just helps me focus my thoughts on Him. You could also say, along with Samuel: "Speak, for your servant is listening" (1 Samuel 3:10). You may even find it helpful to open your hands, as if you are ready to receive something.

This is what I discovered: listening to God is quite hard at first. It takes time, but God *will* speak (see Chapter Two for more on how God speaks). He wants to speak to you, and the more you really listen, the more He will speak.

I suggest you keep a journal of what you've heard, the impressions you've received and anything you've felt God say to you. As I've looked back at mine over the years, I have constantly been surprised how the same themes have reoccurred, or how God has reminded me of something He said so clearly months or even years earlier.

Before we left our church in Newcastle for our ill-fated move to the Midlands, God appeared to be saying that it was going to be a 'stepping stone'. This theme recurred several times. In fact, just before we left Newcastle I attended a ministers' fraternal at a church in Blyth that I had never set foot in before, and there on the wall was a massive mural of (you guessed it!) stepping stones.

Shortly after our departure from the church in the Midlands, a friend reminded me of the stepping stones pictures we had received. That was a great help and encouragement to us during our period of waiting, and of course the move from the Midlands to Banbury was only around forty miles – a short stepping stone in distance.

It really is worth setting time aside to wait on God. You can just block out an hour or go on a full-blown retreat. There are lots of Christian retreat centres dotted around the UK (and the world).

Take a full day or an overnight stay. Go with no agenda, except to meet with God and listen to His voice.

9. Pray when you don't feel like praying!

I run three times a week, pretty much every week. This can be quite a challenge for me. Like everyone else, I'm busy and I'm not getting any younger! I could be doing so many other things with my free time. Sometimes I'm tired and it's cold, wet and windy, but somehow I force myself to get my kit on, do some stretches and head outside. Many times I have forced myself to set out, even though every bit of me wanted to stay in my warm, dry home.

However, the rewards are more than worth it. I return home feeling invigorated, and actually some of my best and most enjoyable runs have happened on those occasions when I've forced myself to go, despite my feelings. In fact, God has sometimes spoken to me, brought direction or given me a sermon outline while I was out running.

It's the same with prayer. The truth is, we have an enemy who will do everything he can to stop us praying (because he knows how powerful it is). However, the rewards are there if we will continue to press through, even when we don't feel like it. Some of my best prayer times have been the ones when I didn't feel like it but I prayed anyway.

If we will discipline ourselves to pray, especially at those times, and even when we have run out of things to pray, we will often find ourselves rewarded by God for seeking Him.

Doesn't the Bible say something about that somewhere?

"And without faith it is impossible to please God, because anyone who comes to him must believe that he exists and that he rewards those who earnestly seek him" (Hebrews 11:6).

10. Ask others to "pray you through"

As a pastor I have committed to praying people through difficult seasons on many occasions. I have prayed people through illness, into new jobs and homes, through exams and debt, through marital problems and even through into the conception of a child. We have an important role to play in praying for one another.

Right now, in this challenging season, why not prayerfully choose and approach people you trust to carry you in prayer each and every day throughout this season? People who will pray persistently until you come through it. It was a massive encouragement for me personally, throughout the waiting season, to know that others were encouraging us and standing with us in prayer. This is the body of Christ at its best, praying and supporting one another in times of need.

Why wait any longer to pray?

Why do we so often use prayer as a last resort when God wants it to be our first port of call? So often we pray when we've exhausted all other options. We spend hours leaning on our own understanding (see Proverbs 3:5-6) and get nowhere; we have sleepless nights tossing and turning, and wake up feeling even more tired and grumpy; we spend time trying to resolve things in our own strength; we talk to as many of our friends as will listen... and still no resolution!

God wants us to turn to prayer *first*. To seek the One who will be found. To talk to the One with the answers, with the solutions, with the comfort, wisdom, revelation and strength. The One who opens doors and who can change our situation in a moment. The One who is, was and evermore shall be.

There is nothing we can do that will benefit us more than prayer. Think about that for a moment. So often we busy ourselves doing anything other than pray, but that doesn't make any sense. Don't wait any longer. Put this book down and get down to some praying. Yes, now! The prayer below may help.

Prayer

Lord, in this waiting season, please help me to pray – especially when I'm struggling to pray, weary of praying or don't know what to pray. Pray with me and through me. Teach me to pray.

Help me to set regular time aside just to worship, sit in Your presence and talk to You. Help me to prioritise fellowship with You during this season, for You are my strength, my provider, my protector, my healer and my sustainer.

Help me not to panic but to pray; to exchange all my troubles, fears and anxieties for Your peace; and to cultivate a relationship with Your Holy Spirit. Help me to be thankful for everything I have rather than disappointed by the things I *don't* have.

Teach me how to hear and recognise Your voice. Please speak to me clearly and lead me into all that You have planned and purposed for me.

Father, as I commit myself to praying, waiting and trusting, help me to go deeper with You and to find all I need in You during this in-between season. In Jesus' name. Amen

Discussion questions for small groups

What have you discovered about prayer from Part One of this book?

What is your daily routine when it comes to prayer and spending time with God? What works for you? How do you fit prayer into a busy routine (especially if you have a demanding job and/or a busy household)? Any tips?

How do you feel about your prayer life? Do you feel it could be better? If so, in which ways?

Have you ever had an experience of deep fellowship with God? Share what occurred at that moment. Can you provide any helpful suggestions for others in the group?

How does God speak to us? Have you ever experienced God speaking really clearly to you about something? Share what happened. How did you know it was God?

What would your next step be in moving into a closer relationship with the Lord?

Is there anyone in the group who needs praying through a challenging situation?

---

1. C. H. Spurgeon, 'Order and Argument in Prayer', The Spurgeon Center, 15 July 1866: (accessed 14 August 2023).

2. S. Chadwick, The Collected Works of Samuel Chadwick, Kindle edition (Jawbone Digital: 2012) p. 98.

3. C. H. Spurgeon, 'The Secret of Power in Prayer', The Spurgeon Center, 8 January 1888: (accessed 14 August 2023).

Part Two

"I wait for the Lord, my whole being waits, and in his word I put my hope. I wait for the Lord more than watchmen wait for the morning, more than watchmen wait for the morning" (Psalms 130:5-6)

Chapter Four

Wait

Londoners don't like waiting. I was recently in the capital and was reminded of this. In fact, on the tube, on the roads and in the shopping centres they take no prisoners. People rarely move out of your way or allow you to go first. There is no messing at all. If you're a tourist like me with no idea where you are going, and you stand still for a moment, you are likely to get flattened. Londoners don't like waiting!

To be fair, none of us like waiting. Who enjoys queueing at the checkout, being on hold with a call centre for several hours or waiting for a takeaway to arrive? Yet waiting is a massive part of our lives. I'm sure you can imagine what those fourteen months without a job were like for me and Julia. Waiting. Waiting. Waiting. (And, I may add, lots of praying and trusting, too.)

The in-between season

Waiting could be described as the in-between season. I'm sure the disciples experienced this during the period between Jesus' death and resurrection, and again following His ascension. They'd had such incredible times with Jesus, listened to life-changing teaching and seen amazing healings, miracles and deliverance. They had seen the supernatural take place and multitudes come to salvation. And yet they had little idea of what would come next.

The in-between season must have been a time of vulnerability, uncertainty, anxiety and fear for them. It must also have been quite traumatic. They must have felt as if they had lost everything, and they had probably also forgotten some of the promises Jesus had made about what was to come next. We, too, can lose sight of what God has promised during the in-between season.

After three years of constantly being with Jesus they must have wondered what to do next. *Is that it? Show's over? What do we do now?* Understandably, some of them – Simon Peter included – went back to what they knew best, the fishing business. And after a night of fishing without catching anything, they found Jesus waiting on the shores of Lake Galilee (see John 21), preparing breakfast for them.

Imagine Jesus making breakfast for you. It must have been delicious! Shortly after they had eaten, Jesus had quite an intense conversation with Simon Peter and asked him three times whether he loved Him, which resulted in Peter being forgiven, accepted and reinstated as a disciple and leader of the group. Peter's short waiting season ended with him being reassigned. What an encouraging end to a waiting season.

During our own in-between season there were times of restlessness, anxiety, fear, uncertainty, frustration, discouragement, disappointment, disillusionment and even despair. There were also moments of anger, grief, resentment, bitterness and depression. I began to lose confidence in myself and even started to question my calling.

I wondered whether I should just give up the stresses and strains of ministry and become a van driver or retrain to do something else. I began to ask God again what He wanted me to do with the rest of my life.

The monotony and lack of employment really took its toll on me. This is an extract from my journal at the time:

Lord – when will this wilderness end for us? No job. No money. No sense of where or what you want us to do. I can't hear your voice. Feel lost. I'm fed up with simply trusting. It's been a year now. We've had barely any income the past two months and again have had to use our savings. When will this ever end????

Pretty much every day I would wake up (being an eternal optimist) and think, *Today will be the day!* And then nothing again. No calls. No emails. No door opening. No job opportunity. Nothing. Just silence. *How long, O God, before you lift us out of this?*

Hide and seek with God

"I will wait for the Lord, who is hiding his face from the descendants of Jacob. I will put my trust in him" (Isaiah 8:17).

I began to wonder whether God was playing hide and seek, although I'd long since counted up to one hundred and there appeared to be no sign of Him! It seemed to me that He was doing all the hiding and I was doing all the seeking, and that the hiding had gone on for too long and was getting beyond a joke.

One of the mysteries of the Christian faith is why God does not appear to intervene in our affairs at certain times, while on other occasions He appears more than willing. Why is this? I don't know the answer to this conundrum, of course, but I would say this: if God appears to be hiding or absent right now, the most important thing you can do is trust Him. Deeply and unequivocally.

We're in good company. Some of the greatest figures in the Bible had to wait to see what God had promised come to pass. Abraham waited until he was ninety-nine for his heir and the child of promise, Isaac.

"When God made his promise to Abraham, since there was no one greater for him to swear by, he swore by himself, saying, 'I will surely bless you and give you many descendants.' And so after waiting patiently, Abraham received what was promised" (Hebrews 6:13-15).

Jacob waited seven years for Rachel and had to work another seven years to settle that debt (see Genesis 29). Moses waited forty years before he was finally trusted by God to lead Israel out of Egypt (see Acts 7). Joseph spent many years as a slave and in prison for a crime he didn't commit before God appointed him prime minister of Egypt (see Genesis 37-41). Hannah waited years to become pregnant with Samuel (see 1 Samuel 1). David waited forty years for the kingship (see 2 Samuel 2-5). Simeon waited many years to meet the Messiah (see Luke 2). One disabled man waited at the pool in Bethesda for an angel to stir the waters (see John 5), while another waited at the gate called Beautiful (see Acts 3). The list goes on.

Ann Voskamp describes waiting like this:

"Waiting is just a gift of time in disguise – a time to pray wrapped up in a ribbon of patience – is the Lord ever late?"[1]

Waiting can seem interminable, but I've discovered that God's timing is always perfect. Paul writes:

"But when the fullness of the time had come, God sent forth His Son, born of a woman, born under the law, to redeem those who were under the law, that we might receive the adoption as sons" (Galatians 4:4-5, NKJV).

God has an uncanny habit of being bang on time. It's infuriating. Never early and never late, but perfectly on time. Somehow, we have to find a way to trust Him during that waiting time. It is almost always longer than we anticipate, but God knows best.

"Here's what I've learned through it all: Don't give up; don't be impatient; be entwined as one with the Lord. Be brave and courageous, and never lose hope. Yes, keep on waiting – for he will never disappoint you!" (Psalms 27:14, TPT).

I've been pastoring the church in Banbury for nearly two years now. The opportunity wasn't there until almost a year into our wilderness period, so we had to wait for it to become available. God kept us waiting until the right door opened. During that period there were other doors and other opportunities, but nothing was the right fit for us or for the church in the season of rebuilding they were in. God knew what He was doing.

If you're waiting right now, here's a promise for you:

I waited and waited and waited some more, patiently, knowing God would come through for me. Then, at last, he bent down and listened to my cry. He stooped down to lift me out of danger from the desolate pit I was in, out of the muddy mess I had fallen into. Now he's lifted me up into a firm, secure place and steadied me while

I walk along his ascending path. A new song for a new day rises up in me every time I think about how he breaks through for me! Ecstatic praise pours out of my mouth until everyone hears how God has set me free. Many will see his miracles; they'll stand in awe of God and fall in love with him! (Psalms 40:1-3, TPT)

Why the wait?

Whatever it is you are waiting for, could it be possible that God is causing you to wait because that perfect opportunity isn't quite ready yet? Rushing into something else would mean missing out on all that God has for you right now. Could it be that God has allowed this moment to cause you to reflect, and that He actually wants to take you in an entirely different direction? Perhaps He wants to do a new thing in you, and He has new plans and purposes for your life. That's exciting and daunting all in one!

Perhaps during this waiting season God wants to work *on* and *in* you. Perhaps this is a preparation and pruning time. When I was first called to ministry I remember my pastor saying that I was "clearly called by God but had some rough edges that needed smoothing down". How rude! But he was right, and I suspect that God is still working on one or two of them.

Perhaps, like me, you have some rough edges that need smoothing out or some long-standing character issues that need to be addressed. I've realised it's better to work with God in these areas or we end up experiencing a prolonged wait. God is in no rush when it comes to refining our character. Do you have any character flaws or sinful habits that you need God to help you with before you move out of the waiting room into what He has next for you?

Perhaps your waiting season has been particularly dark. However, there are some things that can only be discovered in the dark. God spoke through Isaiah, saying:

"And I will give you treasures hidden in the darkness— secret riches. I will do this so you may know that I am the Lord, the God of Israel, the one who calls you by name" (Isaiah 45:3, NLT).

As we reflect on the narrative of the Bible, we discover that Moses' forty days and nights on the mountain (see Exodus 32), Job's experiences of grief and loss (see Job), Joseph in prison (see Genesis 39), Elijah's time on Mount Carmel when he wanted to die (see 1 Kings 18) and Paul's experiences in the desert (see Galatians 1) weren't wasted experiences... they were all part of God's plans and purposes.

It was during some of my darkest days that I received the most precious insights and revelations. So perhaps it's time to develop some night vision, allowing God to reveal the hidden treasures and teach you things you can only discover in the darkness. Remember that:

"Weeping may last through the night, but joy comes with the morning" (Psalms 30:5 NLT).

The waiting season is one of growth and development. During this time we are honed, refined and brought to a new level of maturity in our faith so we can become the people God created us to be and are fully equipped for all He has planned for us. As Pete Scazzero puts it:

"When you are waiting, you're doing the most important thing you can do in life – growing up and becoming the person God created you to be."[2]

Keep your heart right

Perhaps the circumstances you find yourself in are a direct result of other people's actions. You may well be feeling hurt, angry, bitter and aggrieved, and perhaps you even want to take revenge. In these moments, it's important to remember the words of the apostle Paul:

"For we are not fighting against flesh-and-blood enemies, but against evil rulers and authorities of the unseen world, against mighty powers in this dark world, and against evil spirits in the heavenly places" (Ephesians 6:12, NLT).

You must somehow choose to forgive those who have caused you such pain, suffering and loss. I appreciate that for some this may not seem possible right now. I have seen the damage people have caused one another and the incredible pain that abuse, betrayal, abandonment and affairs can have. I'm aware that this journey takes time, but with God's help, and with the support of trusted family members and friends, you can navigate a way through.

Remember that your battle was never, and is never, against flesh and blood, against people, groups, companies or even a Christian denomination. There is only one enemy: the devil. He is the one to get angry with. His scheming causes so many of our problems, but his time will come. Remember the end of the story (see Revelation 20:10).

Somehow, and with God's help, we must choose to forgive and show grace, recognising that we, too, get things wrong, make bad calls, overreact and sin against others. If we're honest for a moment, we will recognise that we are all far from perfect.

One of the verses that continually ministered to me during that wilderness season was this:

"Be still before the LORD and wait patiently for him; do not fret when people succeed in their ways, when they carry out their wicked schemes" (Psalms 37:7).

Over the years, Julia and I have had to choose to forgive others many times and to focus, as best we can, on keeping our hearts right.

"Above all else, guard your heart, for everything you do flows from it" (Proverbs 4:23).

It was a long wait for us, and I guess if you're reading this right now you are more than likely in a season of waiting as well. Let me encourage you, as you wait, to make time to be still, to quieten your heart before Him and to embrace this waiting season that He, by His sovereign choice, has decided to allow you to pass through.

The wait won't last forever

My youngest daughter used to keep me waiting for what seemed like an eternity at the front door whenever I was taking her anywhere. I would call upstairs and tell her to get a move on, and she would reply, "I'm coming." The only problem with her response was that she wasn't actually coming. In fact, she wasn't anywhere close!

However, the promise of God is that He has heard our cry and is on His way (see Psalm 34:17). Be assured of that. One day He will come through for you. It may not always look as you anticipated, but God has a plan that He is executing.

The promise from Lamentations at the beginning of this book reminds us to "keep a grip on hope". Why? Because:

"God's loyal love couldn't have run out, his merciful love couldn't have dried up. They're created new every morning. How great your faithfulness! I'm sticking with God (I say it over and over). He's all I've got left. God proves to be good to the man who passionately waits, to the woman who diligently seeks. It's a good thing to quietly hope, quietly hope for help from God" (Lamentations 3:22-27, MSG).

---

1. A. Voskamp, Twitter, 22 July 2016: https://twitter.com/AnnVoskamp/status/756541901382176768?lang=en (accessed 14 August 2023).

2. P. Scazzero, Twitter, 18 July 2023: (accessed 14 August 2023).

Chapter Five

What waiting teaches us

G od is in charge

One of the things we discover as we wait for God is that nothing we do can force His hand. He is in charge. We can pray, fast, seek and cry out to Him, but God is God. He does as He pleases. His purposes will stand.

This is certainly a lesson I needed to learn during my younger years as a Christian. The waiting season is often a time when God actually allows us to be brought to our knees in order for us to recognise who is in charge (yes, it's true).

I guess of all the people in the Bible, Job was thrown the worst possible curveballs. God allowed Job to be tested by the devil and he lost everything he had (see Job 1:13-22) and experienced immense pain and suffering. Yet although he never gave up hope that God would one day restore all that he had lost (see Job 23:10), he actually questioned God. During his waiting time, God brought Job to a place of submission and worship. Job discovered that God is sovereign, and that there was a lot more to Him and to running the world than he had perhaps anticipated. God demonstrated to Job who was in charge!

As Isaiah reminds us:

"Remember the former things, those of long ago; I am God, and there is no other; I am God, and there is none like me. I make known the end from the beginning, from ancient times, what is still to come. I say, 'My purpose will stand, and I will do all that I please'"

Sometimes God will use our waiting time to remind us that He's in charge and not us – and that He is certainly not at our beck and call. He is sovereign, and He is the one who determines our destiny, not us. He will change things in His perfect timing rather than in our imperfect timing. Sometimes we simply have to step back and let God be God. It can be a humbling experience, but the promise remains:

"If you bow low in God's awesome presence, he will eventually exalt you as you leave the timing in his hands" (1 Peter 5:6, TPT).

God sees things differently from us

"For my thoughts are not your thoughts, neither are your ways my ways,' declares the Lord. 'As the heavens are higher than the earth, so are my ways higher than your ways and my thoughts than your thoughts" (Isaiah 55:8-9).

Here's the thing: God sees the big picture, and as a result there will be times in our lives when He most definitely sees things differently from us. Perhaps God has a different, bigger or better plan than you are anticipating. Maybe the place you are in is crucial to where God is taking you. Try not to become frustrated by this season. Could it be that God has a purpose in you being where you are right now? Please take a moment to reflect on this.

As we were reminded earlier, God knows the plans He has for us (see Jeremiah 29:11). No matter what we can see or are experiencing right now, no matter how dark and challenging things may appear, God most certainly has plans for us. They are plans to prosper us and not to harm us; to give us a hope and a future.

Waiting challenges us. It asks the question, where does your security really lie? And do you really trust in God? OK, so prove it while you wait!

"Sometimes faith means doing nothing. You just stand still, you wait, and you trust. If you try to do something about it, it puts control back in your court" (Rick Warren).[1]

The question is, will we obey God during the waiting season? Waiting is a commitment to continue living in obedience until He speaks or moves. Sometimes I wonder whether God is testing us to see how we will respond and whether we will simply wait for Him to come through.

Abraham couldn't wait for Sarah to have a child, so he went his own way and had Ishmael (see Genesis 16), which led not only to conflict within the family, but also to hostility in Israel and beyond (see Genesis 25:12-18). Esau couldn't wait to eat, and he lost his inheritance to Jacob as a result (see Genesis 25:29-34). The children of

Israel constantly disobeyed God while they waited in the wilderness for the land of promise, and as a result they had to wander for far longer than they should have (see Numbers 14:34).

Let me encourage you to trust God and embrace this season, and to: "Be still before the Lord and wait patiently for him" (Psalms 37:7) because He undoubtedly sees things differently from you.

God is our provider

Early one morning as I sat talking to God in my favourite chair, looking out into our garden, I watched the birds happily eating their breakfast at our bird table and was reminded that, just as his eye is on the sparrow and He provides for all His creatures, He has promised to provide for each one of us:

"Look at the birds of the air; they do not sow or reap or store away in barns, and yet your heavenly Father feeds them. Are you not much more valuable than they?" (Matthew 6:26).

"Are not two sparrows sold for a penny? Yet not one of them will fall to the ground outside your Father's care. And even the very hairs of your head are all numbered. So don't be afraid; you are worth more than many sparrows" (Matthew 10:29-31).

During our waiting season we were reminded that God is our provider and that we would have to rely on Him totally for everything we needed. Neither of us had jobs. We did not belong to a local church family. He had to be enough.

We discovered that we could trust Him to be our peace and provide for us in every way. He kept the wolf from the door. Sometimes it was a challenge financially, but we learned to look to Him constantly. He was and is our provider, and He is also your provider during the waiting season.

"I lift up my eyes to the mountains – where does my help come from? My help comes from the Lord, the Maker of heaven and earth" (Psalms 121:1-2).

The question is: in which direction are you looking? Let me encourage you not to look to man, but rather to the God who is your provider. He will never let you down. There may be moments when you wonder what He is doing, but He will come through for you.

And here's a little secret. While you wait, be generous to others and keep giving to God's work. He loves to see us demonstrate faith during a season of lack. We never stopped tithing or being generous to others during our waiting and jobless season. Julia baked lots of cakes during the lockdowns, and they were a source of joy and refreshment to our neighbours and friends. God provided in every way and, at times, blessed us beyond measure.

How to grow in patience and perseverance

"Be patient, then, brothers and sisters, until the Lord's coming. See how the farmer waits for the land to yield its valuable crop, patiently waiting for the autumn and spring rains" (James 5:7).

Last summer we were stuck in a queue on the M5 for several hours as we returned from our holiday in Wales. We were literally a thirty-minute drive from our home. It was so frustrating! Most of us hate waiting. We want everything instantly. Now, now, now! However, that's not how God works, and the waiting season is when we really learn how to be patient.

The Collins Online Dictionary says that patience "implies the bearing of suffering, provocation, delay, tediousness, etc. with calmness, perseverance and self-control". It finds its origin in the Old French from Latin "*patientia* endurance", with "*pati-*" meaning "to suffer".[2]

I discovered during the waiting season that God wanted me to patiently persevere. In fact, patience is one of the core characteristics of a Christian. It is a fruit of the Spirit. I realised God still had some work to do in my life! Perseverance is produced when our faith is tested, and is necessary for us to become mature in God's eyes.

"Consider it pure joy, my brothers and sisters, whenever you face trials of many kinds, because you know that the testing of your faith produces perseverance. Let perseverance finish its work so that you may be mature and complete, not lacking anything" (James 1:2-4).

I can't say the season was always joyful, but in the midst of waiting we knew that God was at work, honing and refining us for His glory. We trusted Him in that.

Our faith and trust in God are tested when we have to wait. And when what we have been waiting for materialises, our faith increases. We rejoice at His faithfulness and provision. I'm more and more convinced that He allows us to wait at times in order to increase our dependency on Him and to build our faith.

God wants His people to be strong, resilient and faith-filled. He will quietly go about building faith and trust in us, because He knows what lies ahead. He is aware of the different challenges and purposes He has preordained for our lives, and knows that without a strong faith we will be unable to flourish.

To be fruitful in a season of suffering and lack

We've already mentioned Joseph, who was sold into slavery, falsely accused of rape and thrown into prison, but who eventually became prime minister of Egypt.

Joseph could have been completely paralysed by all he had experienced and spent his days feeling sorry for himself while he waited for justice. However, he chose to be fruitful.

"Joseph named his firstborn Manasseh and said, 'It is because God has made me forget all my trouble and all my father's household.' The second son he named Ephraim and said, 'It is because God has made me fruitful in the land of my suffering'" (Genesis 41:51-52).

In his later years, Joseph's father Jacob described him like this:

"Joseph is a fruitful vine, a fruitful vine near a spring, whose branches climb over a wall. With bitterness archers attacked him; they shot at him with hostility. But his bow remained steady, his strong arms stayed supple, because of the hand of the Mighty One of Jacob, because of the Shepherd, the Rock of Israel, because of your father's God, who helps you, because of the Almighty, who blesses you with blessings of the skies above, blessings of the deep springs below, blessings of the breast and womb." (Genesis 49:22-25)

This man – born to lead and full of vision – experienced coercion and confinement three times, yet he kept his heart right and determined that he would still serve others and be fruitful.

Trials, struggles and problems can rob us of courage and disable us from having a normal life and ministry, ultimately destroying our ability to be fruitful. However, we have a choice. We can choose to allow despair, frustration and discouragement to negatively impact our lives, or we can choose fruitfulness instead. Jesus chose and appointed us to bear fruit that would last (John 15:16), regardless of our circumstances.

God wants you and me to be fruitful while we wait. So don't waste the wait! Don't be passive during your wait. I determined that I would make my waiting season count, so during that period I completed and published my second book, helped Julia write her first, started work on my third book, revised my website, recorded all the chapters from my first book, *Imagine*, on YouTube for small groups to use, updated old blog posts and developed my social media ministry. I also found some time to minister in person, to read and to disciple others.

Determine in your heart to make this waiting season count! Use the time well. Be fruitful.

Waiting causes us to re-evaluate our lives

"Teach us to realise the brevity of life, so that we may grow in wisdom" (Psalm 90:12).

This was the verse my father chose for his funeral. He wanted to remind everyone that life is short and that we should be wise in using the time we have well. Our waiting season creates an opportunity for us to pause, to reflect, to gain wisdom, and to consider and perhaps reset our lives.

We could also ask God if there is anything we need to learn from the past season, anything we could have done differently or better, anything He would like to highlight or change. If we use the waiting time well, we will ask questions such as:

- What wasn't working back then?

- How can I live differently?

- What should my (or our) future priorities be – spiritually, emotionally, physically, relationally, financially and vocationally?

- What and who is God calling me (or us) to be?

- What would I regret not doing, or at least attempting to do, before I die?

A season of waiting can often prove to be a pivotal moment in our lives. A moment to stop, reset and start again. An opportunity to start the next season with clarity about the way God intends us to live.

God often prunes and prepares us for what's next

Now, I'm not an expert gardener – in fact, I shouldn't be allowed anywhere near a plant bed! My forte is lawn cutting. I love a neat and tidy lawn with great tram line stripes. Plants I know little about; however, I do know there are times when a gardener (usually my wife) has to prune and prepare plants for the next season. Waiting time isn't wasted time, it's valuable working time. God never wastes the waiting seasons and is always at work in our lives.

Are you struggling to understand the season you're in? I've been there, done that and got the T-shirt (more than once!). Everything was going so well for us before this most recent wilderness experience, then suddenly a large curveball arrived. Certainly in our case, it felt like everything had been taken away. For fourteen months, pretty much all the things we had been called and gifted to do, the things we had been fruitful in, were gone. There was virtually nothing left. If only God had given us some sort of warning that pruning was about to occur!

"He lops off every branch that doesn't produce. And he prunes those branches that bear fruit for even larger crops" (John 15:2, TLB).

For our part, we must learn to submit to the pruning process. Pruning involves cutting off the dead branches and cutting back the living branches. Both elements are necessary for the tree to flourish and to stimulate new growth. When God prunes, He doesn't mess around. He does it for our best, so we can be more fruitful.

As I look back on that period now, I can see that God was cutting back the parts that were unfruitful, sinful and superficial. He did some resetting and even pruned the areas that were fruitful and productive in order that they would become more fruitful again. It wasn't a pleasant experience, but I have certainly benefited from the pruning process – and I hope those around me have too!

You may be wondering what on earth is happening right now. You may have said something like, "Lord, what is going on? I've been faithful and have sown into your kingdom, but I've been made redundant from this job I loved," or, "I've invested my life in this really successful ministry and now it's just not happening," or, "Why have you allowed this dream role to end? It was my life, and I was being so fruitful!" or, "Why has this relationship ended?" or, "You clearly lead me into this new role, and nothing is happening. Why, Lord, have you allowed this?"

You may feel really mad at God. You may be wondering whether He actually loves and cares for you. You may even feel as if you're being punished, but of course that isn't true. Pruning must never be confused with punishment. We should never equate the two.

Perhaps the Master Gardener has His pruning shears in His hand right now, but rest assured that He loves you and that He sees you as someone who can bear significantly more fruit than you currently are. Pruning is part of the discipleship process – it's part and parcel of our spiritual growth – but it always results in more fruitfulness, and brings greater glory to God.

"When you produce much fruit, you are my true disciples. This brings great glory to my Father" (John 15:8, NLT).

God prepares us for what is to come

"So, we are convinced that every detail of our lives is continually woven together for good, for we are his lovers who have been called to fulfil his designed purpose. For he knew all about us before we were born, and he destined us from the beginning to share the likeness of his Son. This means the Son is the oldest among a vast family of brothers and sisters who will become just like him" (Romans 8:28-29, TPT).

If we believe that God has a plan and a purpose for us, and that our lives are intricately woven together, we can accept that waiting time is often preparation time. King David waited forty years to become king of Israel, and I'm sure that not a single second was wasted by

God as He honed and refined David's character and leadership skills, so that, when the time was right, he could lead Israel well.

Joseph may have felt that his time working for Potiphar and then being abandoned in prison under a false charge was wasted time for a man with a calling to lead a nation. However, as we touched on earlier, we can be sure that Joseph was learning humility, empathy and compassion, and developing his leadership and people skills.

Your current job or circumstances may not be your dream or even your destiny, but you can be sure that God is using this time as a preparation for what He has in mind for you. Difficult as it may be to accept, He has you right where He wants you in this season – and there is a good reason for it.

So stay faithful to God and try to embrace this season. Ask Him what He wants you to do right now. He knows your future and everything that lies ahead. Study, read, learn, prepare and address the issues that constantly trip you up. Do the prep now, because one day you will look back and be able to see that God has been directing your steps and preparing you for what lies ahead. Don't underestimate what He is doing during this season of waiting.

The question is: what would He have you do now so that you are absolutely ready for when He opens that door?

Waiting is a preordained season

"Your eyes saw my unformed body; all the days ordained for me were written in your book before one of them came to be" (Psalms 139:16).

These are mind-blowing words! Could it be that this season of praying, waiting and trusting is a preordained season? That (whisper it!) God preordained it all along? On the one hand, that's a tad frustrating. *Why, Lord?* But on the other hand, it means He must have a plan and a purpose... and it will be for good!

Let's get things into perspective. Life is full seasons, and sometimes we will find ourselves in a waiting season. The question is this: how will you and I respond? Will we have a major tantrum and throw ourselves onto the floor, rolling around and screaming like a Premier League footballer after a light tackle? Or will we accept and embrace the God-ordained season we find ourselves in?

What if God is keeping you in that workplace or neighbourhood because He wants you to be salt and light, to minister His grace and love, or to share your faith with someone who doesn't yet know Him? Perhaps you have an assignment to complete – even if it's in a place you don't want to be – before God opens the next door? Have you asked Him if there is anything He wants you to do where He has placed you?

Early on in our waiting season, I felt God whisper in my ear, "I ordained this. Make the most of it! Use it well. Don't waste it!"

---

1. R. Warren, 'God Is All-Powerful – So You Don't Have to Be', Pastor Rick, 8 September 2021: (accessed 14 August 2023).

2. 'Patience', Collins Online Dictionary: (accessed 14 August 2023).

Chapter Six

What not to do while you wait

One of the challenges of waiting for any length of time is the desire to just do something... anything! We become so desperate for movement, change or any kind of development. However, Solomon warns us that:

"Impatience will get you into trouble. Some people ruin themselves by their own stupid actions and then blame the Lord" (Proverbs 19:2-3, GNT)

So what *shouldn't* we do while we wait?

Don't rush into making any decisions

Isn't hindsight a wonderful thing? As I look back on the decision I made to take up my previous pastorate, I recognise it was rushed, and that we were rushed into accepting the position by others. It was the right decision to leave the church we had been leading, but we moved to the wrong church at the wrong moment with the wrong people. We were a poor fit. We are still living with the consequences of that poor, rushed decision. Don't rush! Don't settle for Ishmael when Isaac, the child of promise, awaits.

Thankfully, God is sovereign and factors in our stupidity. He is more than able to work around our mistakes and guide us through into His blessings and purposes. God can turn our past poor choices and failures into future successes. He really can – I have personally experienced it.

A word of warning when a door finally opens, a breakthrough appears to have happened or a new job or relationship appears to be on the horizon: take your time. Don't rush into any major decisions without serious, prayerful thought and consideration. Just because a door is open, that doesn't mean it's the right one for you. Slow down. Stop and look back. How did the hasty, prayerless decisions you made in the past turn out? Only fools rush in.

We live in a crazy, fast-paced world of rush, where everyone around us is trying to get as much done as possible, as quickly as possible, so we sometimes miss the quiet, gentle voice and timing of the Spirit. Seek God. Do due diligence. Investigate. Sleep on it. Ask others to pray. Trust God that if it's right He won't let you miss it.

"Get all the advice you can, and you will succeed; without it you will fail" (Proverbs 15:22, GNT).

Don't trust your own limited understanding or judgement. Seek the wise counsel of others – especially those who won't necessarily agree with you, and who will speak honestly into your life – and ask God to lead and guide you with absolute clarity. Ask Him to close any wrong doors. Check your heart. Are you disturbed or do you have a sense of peace? Have there been confirmations? Don't rush into anything until you are absolutely sure that God has spoken.

"Since we are living by the Spirit, let us follow the Spirit's leading in every part of our lives" (Galatians 5:25, NLT).

As followers of Jesus, let's make sure we are following rather than leading. We must learn to position ourselves behind the Spirit, never ahead of Him; always following wherever He leads. He knows best. When in doubt, wait.

"The circumstances of our lives are to us an infallible indication of God's will, when they concur with the inward promptings of the Holy Spirit and with the Word of God. So long as they are stationery, wait. When you must act, they will open, and a way will be made through the oceans and rivers, wastes and rocks. If you do not know what you ought to do, stand still until you do" (F. B. Meyer).[1]

Don't try to force open doors that are closed!

Sometimes if we've been waiting for something for what seems like a long time and God doesn't appear to be responding, we can be tempted to take matters into our own hands. King Saul couldn't wait for the prophet Samuel to arrive, or for the priests to offer a peace offering to God in order to ensure victory over the Philistines, so he usurped the priestly role and offered the sacrifice himself (see 1 Samuel 13:8-14).

When Samuel eventually arrived, he asked Saul why he had done so. Saul replied, "I felt compelled" (see 1 Samuel 13:12, NKJV). The result? "And Samuel said to Saul, 'You have done foolishly... now your kingdom shall not continue'" (13:13-14, NKJV). Saul's impatience, impulsiveness and disobedience cost him his kingdom. He simply couldn't wait for God.

We mentioned Abraham and Sarah earlier. They were growing old (*really* old!) and became vulnerable, as so many of us do, to acting in the flesh rather than waiting for God's promise to be fulfilled. It's interesting that even after the birth of Ishmael they had to wait a further thirteen years for the true heir, Isaac.

We must learn not to strive, not to force anything, but rather to let go, wait and allow God to act in His perfect timing.

"Above all, trust in the slow work of God" (Pierre Teilhard de Chardin).[2]

During our fourteen-month break from ministry with no regular income, I felt under increasing pressure to take on a pastorate. We looked at several churches, yet none appeared to be a fit. The doors that opened quickly closed again. One particular church suddenly closed its doors having done all it could to attract us there in the first place. To this day, no explanation has been given.

This is why it is so important that we learn to allow God to open the doors. God's promise to me and Julia in the waiting season was this: "Behold, I will open a door that no man can shut!" Several times we received these same words from the Lord, and I soon realised there was a door out there that only God could open. This completely released me from the pressure of looking to others or even my own denomination's leaders for the next door to open. I decided to look solely to God to open the right door in His perfect timing.

This was my prayer at the time:

"God, you open doors that no man can shut, and you shut doors that no man can open. I trust you with every door."

Once we had accepted the position in Banbury, we spent several months looking for a house so we could relocate. We saw a house at the right price that looked as if it would have been perfect for us, but for several days we couldn't even get through to the estate agent. I sought God about this, and He whispered into my ear: "Why are you trying to force open a closed door? The hold-up is to force you to wait, as something better is on the horizon. It's all about timing." He was right, and He provided us with a beautiful house in a picturesque village just outside Banbury.

Learn to embrace the closed doors while you wait. God can even make the wrong decisions of the people around you work in your favour. He knows best. He may have just saved you from making a bad choice. Thank Him! As I look back at the doors He has closed, I'm so thankful I can now see His hand at work, leading and guiding my life.

I'm encouraged by these words from Jesus:

"Jesus replied, 'You do not realise now what I am doing, but later you will understand'" (John 13:7).

Remember Joseph. When God wants you in the palace rather than the prison, nothing can stop Him. The resentment of Joseph's brothers, who sold him into slavery, couldn't stop Him. The lies of Potiphar's wife and the butler forgetting him couldn't stop Him. Consider this: God was with Joseph through it all. God ordered his steps from the moment his brothers rejected him until the moment he became prime minister of Egypt.

Thankfully, your destiny is in God's hands, rather than in the hands of people, and He will open the right doors in His perfect timing. Years later, when Joseph finally stood face to face with the brothers who had treated him so badly, he said:

"As for you, you meant evil against me, but God meant it for good, to bring it about that many people should be kept alive, as they are today" (Genesis 50:20, ESV).

Get this... the purposes of God will eventually overcome even the plans of people. No one can prevent the purposes and plans God has ordained for your life. Except you.

Trust God to open the right doors.

Don't wait for a lost cause

This is a really tough one, but you need to be clear from God and in your own mind as to whether the wait you're participating in right now is one he has called you to or whether it's a personal cause you have taken up. Perhaps, and I say this gently, it's time to give up on a lost cause. You will need to hear from God on this. I don't know your situation, but perhaps you should prayerfully review it before Him, talk about it with some wise friends and allow God to speak into your situation.

Perhaps you are waiting for the fulfilment of a promise you believe God gave you many years ago. I've met numerous Christians who have been waiting for God to fulfil His promise to them. In fact, I met one Christian lady who was absolutely convinced that God was going to help her conceive a baby, and that He had even given her a name for the child. Sadly, there were three problems with that: 1) she had no husband (or even a boyfriend, for that matter!); 2) she'd had a hysterectomy several years earlier; and 3) as we gently tried to suggest to her, there had only been one immaculate conception in history, and that was Jesus. But what an unbelievably tragic situation for this lady.

Perhaps now is a good moment to reflect and ask yourself whether you're waiting for a promise God never made. You might be waiting for that person to fall in love with you or for that promotion at work or for that ministry opportunity to open, while God has something so much better for you just around the corner.

As I've counselled people over the years, I've discovered that a lost cause is a really challenging thing to recognise, never mind free yourself from. When you've held on to a perceived promise for a long time and shared it with others, it can be really tough to let it go. However, you must. Why? Because your life is on hold. You are trapped in a false promise and are missing out on everything God really does have for you!

If you're not sure the promise is from God, can I suggest that you surrender it to Him? If it is from God, ask Him to make it absolutely clear and to renew it with you. If it is, He will speak clearly and confirm it several times over, through different people and different means, so you know for sure. At the same time, seek wise counsel from trusted people who know you well.

"Listen well to wise counsel and be willing to learn from correction so that by the end of your life you'll be known for your wisdom. A person may have many ideas concerning God's plan for his life, but only the designs of God's purpose will succeed in the end" (Proverbs 19:20-21, TPT).

Ask yourself: 'Is God waiting for me?'

Perhaps God is waiting for you rather than you waiting for Him. Perhaps He is waiting for you to address or get help with your Achilles heel – the thing that keeps tripping you up and holding you back from fully receiving all that He has for you. Is God waiting for you to be obedient to His Word or to do what He has specifically called you to do? I've discovered over the years that simple acts of obedience often open doors.

Perhaps God is waiting for you to let go and trust Him, so He can lead you into all that He has planned and purposed for you. Perhaps He is waiting for you to take that first step, and then He will back you with all the resources of heaven...

Perhaps God has already said that the time is NOW!

Remember who you are waiting for!

As we conclude this chapter, I want to encourage you with these verses from the start of the chapter:

"I wait for the Lord, my whole being waits, and in his word I put my hope. I wait for the Lord more than watchmen wait for the morning, more than watchmen wait for the morning" (Psalms 130:5-6).

Remember who you are waiting for. You're not waiting for a man, woman, employer, business, bank or doctor... you are waiting for the Lord! And not just any Lord – the King of kings and Lord of lords! So, look to Him and remember this:

"Since ancient times no one has heard, no ear has perceived, no eye has seen any God besides you, who acts on behalf of those who wait for him" (Isaiah 64:4).

Prayer

Father, thank you that You have a plan and purpose for my life. Please help me to trust You deeply during this unsettling season, knowing You will provide all I need. Help me to be at peace; not to strive, but rather to wait patiently for Your intervention or for the next door to open.

Father, work in my heart during this waiting season. Help me to cultivate my relationship with You and to be empowered and equipped by the time I spend in Your precious presence. May I discover how to be still and know that You are God.

Please build faith, hope, trust, patience and perseverance in me. Hone, refine, prune, prepare and reset any areas of my life that require it. I want to be more like Jesus. Help me to keep my heart right, to forgive anyone I need to forgive and to keep my eyes fixed on You. I desire to be fruitful in this season and make the most of it.

And when the time is right to move forward, help me to clearly recognise it and to step boldly into all that you have for me.

While I continue to wait, this is my declaration:

"I remain confident of this: I will see the goodness of the Lord in the land of the living. Wait for the Lord; be strong and take heart and wait for the Lord" (Psalms 27:13-14).

Amen

Discussion questions for small groups

Share your experience of any waiting seasons you have been through.

What were you waiting for, and what did you learn about yourself and about God?

Did you reflect on and reset your life during this time? Did you make any changes?

Have you ever experienced God pruning your life?

Have you ever become aware that you were waiting for a lost cause or that God was actually waiting for you?

How can we make the most of the waiting seasons and be fruitful?

Which particular Bible verses have helped you through these times?

How can we support others in the group while they are navigating through them?

Is there anyone in the group you can commit to praying through their waiting season?

---

1. F. B. Meyer quoted by D. Willard in Hearing God Through the Year (Westmont, IL: IVP, 2004), p. 29.

2. P. Teilhard de Chardin, quoted by dotMagis Editor in 'Prayer of Teilhard de Chardin', Ignatian Spirituality: (accessed 14 August 2023).

Part Three

"Keep trusting in the Lord and do what is right in his eyes. Fix your heart on the promises of God, and you will dwell in the land, feasting on his faithfulness. Find your delight and true pleasure in Yahweh, and he will give you what you desire the most. Give God the right to direct your life, and as you trust him along the way, you'll find he pulled it off perfectly! He will appear as your righteousness, as sure as the dawning of a new day. He will manifest as your justice, as sure and strong as the noonday sun. Quiet your heart in his presence and wait patiently for Yahweh. And don't think for a moment that the wicked, in their prosperity, are better off than you. Stay away from anger and revenge. Keep envy far from you, for it only leads you into lies. For one day the wicked will be destroyed, but those who trust in the Lord will inherit the land." (Psalms 37:3-9 TPT)

Chapter Seven

Trust

"Sometimes we have to wait a long time... during the waiting period, keep on trusting God."[1]

Four years ago, we were happily settled in Newcastle upon Tyne, following our dream. We had swapped our old congregational church building for an enormous four-storey bingo hall and were in the process of refurbishing it. We were building God's Kingdom, ministering to and reaching the people of the East End, and beyond. We were enjoying our busy lives. We loved the city and the people of Newcastle. We were settled where we were, and felt comfortable with our amazing team and the people around us. Our youngest daughter was about to get married to a wonderful young man. Life was full, and we were incredibly fulfilled.

In the space of about ten days, God turned our world upside down. He threw us a massive curveball (or two, actually, as it turns out!) and we received the call to pastor a church in the Midlands.

Julia and I were initially shell-shocked. We had never considered moving, but we both sensed it was time to return to the South. One moment we were settled and committed to building God's Kingdom in Newcastle... the next we were uprooting. Five months later we found ourselves living and ministering in a new city. That's when the second curveball struck. It didn't work out and, as I mentioned before, we were both left unemployed.

As I reflected on this months later, I simply couldn't believe what had happened. Our time in Newcastle had probably been the most fruitful of our entire ministry, and it felt like we had sacrificed so much. We had built a great church, then given up all the precious relationships we had formed, abandoned our youngest daughter and fiancé just months before their wedding, and departed an amazing city with its quayside, shops, beaches and beautiful countryside. I even had to relinquish my Newcastle United season ticket!

Let me tell you, we not only grieved what we'd lost; we grieved even more deeply in the knowledge that we had made such incredible sacrifices only for things not to work out in the Midlands. I guess you could call it a double curveball. *Why, Lord? Why, why, why?*

We need to properly grieve our losses

I'm not one for great introspection; however, I have recognised over the past few years that we often move on from our losses too quickly without grieving them properly. My father died during this difficult season, which coincided with the second UK lockdown. Like so many others who lost loved ones, I wasn't able to see him before he died in hospital. That was incredibly tough. Almost a year later, Julia suggested to me that perhaps I hadn't grieved my father properly. I believe she was right.

Whether it's the loss of a loved one or close friend, or the loss of a career, calling, business or project, we need to recognise that we have suffered a loss. We've taken a hit. We need to grieve.

I've realised since that anger, frustration, resentment and joylessness are often signs that I am grieving something I've lost. When I feel these emotions I need to identify what is going on and then allow myself moments to feel the sadness and express my pain and hurt before God. It's OK to be disappointed with your life. It's OK to feel angry and frustrated. It's OK to feel sad. It's OK to shed some tears. I certainly did.

I believe that part of our healing and restoration comes from identifying our losses in whatever context they arise. We need to properly grieve them. Grief is God's gift to help us navigate the transitions in our lives. Once we have grieved properly, we can move forward in faith, trust and expectation.

God can't always answer the why in the now

As I lay in bed in the middle of the night thinking, pondering, processing and wondering, and wading through the why's, what ifs and maybes, and considering the key decisions, the mistakes I had made and the inevitable regrets, I felt God whisper in my ear, "I can't answer the why in the now."

I believe what God was saying in that moment was: "Simon, I can't explain what I've allowed to happen right now, so you'll just have to trust me. Maintain a simple, childlike trust."

As I've continued to reflect on this over time, I have wondered how many people out there are also wondering what on earth God is doing. *Why have you thrown us these massive curveballs, Lord? Why, oh why?*

No matter what has come your way, make a decision today that you will simply trust Him, because He knows everything about your situation. You may have to accept that you can't know the why in the now, but that God has a plan, and He will sustain and carry you through whatever you are about to face in the days ahead. That knowledge is reassuring and really quite releasing.

You're in good company!

I've already mentioned Joseph, Job and David, but when her husband and two sons died, Naomi must also have wondered, *Why me?* At times, Jeremiah must have wondered why he had been called as a prophet. Jonah and Naaman definitely had their 'why' moments! Esther must have had wondered why she had been chosen to become queen. The disciples must have wondered what was happening following Jesus' death. Paul must have wondered why the Holy Spirit did not permit him to preach the gospel in Asia Minor. We're in good company! We are part of the great company of men and women wondering, *Why, Lord?*

If you are wondering why, choose to trust God. It's easier said than done some days, but it is critical nonetheless. I'm praying for anyone who is struggling with the 'why' that they will trust God and stay close to Him. Place everything in His hands today and ask Him to fill you with the peace that passes all understanding (Philippians 4:7). May it completely fill and guard your heart and mind in Christ Jesus.

You may never get to know why

There are so many things that surprise us in life. Why didn't I get that nailed-down promotion? Why did that door I was sure would open remain shut? Why did that person reject me and let me down? Why did I take that step of faith only for everything to go pear-shaped? Why did the project I'd invested everything in suddenly come to an unexpected end? Why do accidents and disasters happen? Why do people die before their time? Why does life suddenly take a dark and challenging twist sometimes? I think we must accept that we may never fully understand these things this side of eternity.

"For now we see only a reflection as in a mirror; then we shall see face to face. Now I know in part; then I shall know fully, even as I am fully known" (1 Corinthians 13:12).

Sometimes we never get to understand the why in the now, so we must place our lives in the hands of the One who knows all things, and we must make a decision to trust Him while we wait. David, who had learned how to really trust God during his life, declared:

"God, the one and only – I'll wait as long as he says. Everything I hope for comes from him, so why not? He's solid rock under my feet, breathing room for my soul, An impregnable castle: I'm set for life. My help and glory are in God – granite-strength and safe-harbor-God – So trust him absolutely, people; lay your lives on the line for him. God is a safe place to be"

For many Christians, the reality is that we have never really had to trust God for very much until we're thrown a massive curveball. Then we are suddenly, often without warning, forced to trust Him.

In fact, it can be quite easy to live our lives, for the most part, without having to trust and depend on Him.

We all declare that we trust God. We sing about it on Sundays. And most days we can survive... until the day comes when we are really forced to trust Him while we wait for Him to intervene.

Trust God deeply

One of the most popular circus acts is the trapeze artist. I've watched these artists swing back and forth, suspended from the big top with no safety net, and admired how brave (or crazy!) they are. Eventually, the crowd hushes in anticipation as the artist focuses (prays, perhaps) and lets go of the swing to launch themself towards the moving vacant swing. For a moment they are in mid-air with nothing to hold on to. Thankfully, a few seconds later they catch the swing and the crowd breaks out into rapturous applause.

Our in-between waiting season can sometimes feel like that. We can't go back, but we're caught in suspended animation, in mid-air, with nothing to hold on to. We may feel vulnerable, fearful and alone, but rest assured that God has us in His grip. He is, in fact, holding on to us. We can't always feel it or sense Him, but the Bible promises us that "The eternal God is our refuge, and underneath are the everlasting arms" (Deuteronomy 33:27).

As I mentioned earlier, I wrote a book in 2018 entitled *Imagine: Trusting God like never before*, based on the incredible promise we find in Proverbs 3:5-6:

"Trust in the Lord with all your heart and do not lean on your own understanding. In all your ways acknowledge him and he will make your paths straight."

This is such an important promise to hold on to and live out each day, and even more so during your in-between season. I think Julia and I have been inadvertently adding some additional chapters to that book during the waiting period! But seriously, I found myself rereading my own book and relearning some stuff about trusting God.

In fact, my daily prayer was this:

Father, help me to trust you deeply during this unsettling season and to be at peace; not to strive but rather to wait for the next door to open. Help us to recognise it when it does. Amen

---

1. N. Gumbel, Facebook, 10 January 2023: https://www.facebook.com/ni ckygumbel (accessed 14 August 2023).

Chapter Eight

So how do we trust God while we wait?

This is not a rhetorical question. How do we do it in practice? What does everyday trust look like? Here are some tips to help you trust God in the here and now.

Remember what He has done in the past

When the Israelites were facing imminent defeat by the Philistines at Mizpah, the Lord sent out loud thunder from heaven, causing the Philistines to panic, and enabling Israel to defeat them. Samuel wanted Israel to remember the way God had miraculously intervened, so he set up a memorial stone. He named it Ebenezer, saying, 'Thus far the Lord has helped us'" (1 Samuel 7:12).

"Ebenezer" means "stone of help".[1] I've been a Christian since I was a little boy, and God has always been my helper. He and I have a lot of history, so during the waiting season I was able to look back at the many, many times He had been there for me. I recalled numerous miracles of provision, healing, breakthrough, opened doors and answered prayers. He truly is the God who helps us.

I soon realised that the God who had brought us this far was certainly not about to let us down. We just needed to keep praying, waiting and trusting. I was reminded that the God of the Bible is also our God. The God of Abraham, Isaac, Jacob, Moses, Joshua, Ruth, David, Solomon, Esther, Jeremiah, Matthew, Mark, Luke, John, James, Peter and Paul is our God. Isn't that incredible? The God of miracles is our God!

We read the stories of the saints of old and are reminded that He is the same God, and that it is our turn to trust Him now, just as they did. It's our turn to live lives full of faith, expectation and hope, while remaining fully aware that the God who worked in and through these saints is ready and willing to be glorified through our lives in this generation.

Please don't forget what God has done for you in the past. Remind yourself of the times He has rescued and provided for you, and in particular of the breakthroughs and miracles of provision. Yesterday's victories should encourage us as we await today's breakthroughs. The God who brought you this far is not about to fail you now.

Stand on His specific promises to you

"I am counting on the Lord; yes, I am counting on him. I have put my hope in his word" (Psalms 130:5, NLT).

I have already mentioned the importance of standing on God's general promises as we pray. However, God also provides us with specific promises, just for us. Consider the promises He made to Abraham, Isaac, Jacob, Moses, David, Solomon and so many others.

Anyone who has flown anywhere or travelled on a ship will know that there is sometimes turbulence or stormy weather on the way to their destination. Life isn't always a smooth ride. The ship Paul was sailing to Rome on was ravaged by a raging storm that lasted for days. In fact, those aboard began to lose all hope of survival, so ferocious was the storm. In the midst of this, Paul was able to encourage the crew and his fellow travellers with God's promise:

"Last night an angel of the God to whom I belong and whom I serve stood beside me and said, 'Do not be afraid, Paul. You must stand trial before Caesar; and God has graciously given you the lives of all who sail with you.' So keep up your courage, men, for I have faith in God that it will happen just as he told me" (Acts 27:23-25).

God kept His promise and Paul ended up shipwrecked in Malta (there are worse places to be stranded, I suppose!), where the people received the gospel for the first time. Sometimes our in-between seasons provide an opportunity for God to work in ways we never anticipated. Whatever we face, our trust and our hope must stand on the reliable and unchanging Word of God and His promises. That must be our foundation.

Are there any pictures God has given you (remember my stepping stones), or particular promises that have stood out to you – either in His Word or given prophetically – that are relevant to your situation? Any revelations from God you can stand on during this season of praying and waiting and trusting? Like Paul, is there anything God has already promised that you can use as your foundation?

When I was a child, we used to sing a chorus at church about the man who built his house upon the rock. Our lives must be built on the rock (Jesus), on the sure foundation of God's Word and on His incredible promises.

"His divine power has given us everything we need for a godly life through our knowledge of him who called us by his own glory and goodness. Through these he has given us his very great and precious promises, so that through them you may participate in the divine nature, having escaped the corruption in the world caused by evil desires" (2 Peter 1:3-4).

Perhaps in the midst of your praying, waiting and trusting, God has already spoken – but you've missed that still, small voice; you've missed those gentle whispers, those leadings and perhaps even those warnings. Can I suggest that you ask Father God to remind you of what He's already said? There may be some clues there as to what will happen next.

This is why journalling is so important. We need to record our thoughts and prayers, and what we sense God is saying, on an almost daily basis. I have found it such a help to be able to look back. My journal has provided so many 'aha' moments as I've been reminded of what God has already said.

Do what is right in His eyes

"Keep trusting in the Lord and do what is right in his eyes" (Psalm 37:3).

King Asa was one of Israel's few great kings, and the writer of the book of Kings records that "Asa did what was right in the eyes of the Lord, as his father David had done" (1 Kings 15:11). He addressed the sins of his fathers, and dealt with much of what was wrong with Israel at the time. In fact, the writer records that King Asa's heart was "was fully committed to the Lord all his life" (1 Kings 15:14).

One of the things I've discovered in my own walk is that God demands my obedience in all areas of my life: in the small matters and in the issues of great consequence. He doesn't treat them any differently. He wants me to do what is right before Him; to obey Him in public and in private – even when nobody is looking.

I also discovered during my early years as a Christian that there were occasions when God would not allow me to move forward until I had done what He was telling me to do. I've challenged my congregations over the years with the question: "Have you done what God has told you to do yet?"

We often make commitments on a Sunday in response to a sermon, but then Monday morning arrives and we carry on living as if Sunday had never happened. Perhaps God has been on your case about something for a long time. Simple obedience will sometimes create a pathway out of the in-between season, and as we finally submit and obey God, a cry comes from heaven: "At last!"

Breakthrough often comes when we are obedient to God – no matter how insignificant it may appear to us – and do what is right in his eyes. Obedience is a massive declaration of trust and a demonstration that God knows best. Obedience really does have the potential to open a massive door to God's blessing.

Have you done what God has told you to do yet?

Make a choice to leave the past behind

When life throws us an unpleasant curveball and God doesn't appear to be explaining why, and we're not getting the answers we want, it's important that, at the appropriate time, we let go of whatever past situation or issue is troubling us. From personal experience, I believe we must settle it in our hearts (and with God and others, where necessary) and begin to stop looking back. We must refuse to nurse anger, hurts, resentment and regrets, and move into all that God has for us.

My mum used to say, "There's no use crying over spilt milk." That may seem a little insensitive, particularly if you've experienced bereavement, some form of abuse or heart-breaking trauma, and of course you will need time to talk and process what has happened and receive God's healing (see my earlier point about allowing ourselves time to grieve).

However, Julia and I realised that it would be all too easy to keep going over the events we had experienced, picking them apart and sharing them with everyone who had time to listen. The result of doing this is that we remain stuck where God does not want us to dwell. If we're not careful, we will not only bring ourselves down each time we revisit those things, but we will have the same impact on those listening.

It takes real discipline to choose to shut that topic down each time someone attempts to revisit it and say, "Right now, I'm leaving the past behind and moving into all that God has for me. I'm believing for better things because God is on my side."

Julia and I had to make a conscious decision to stop revisiting the past and to trust God with our future. Some of us will find this easier than others, depending on what we have experienced. You may need to seek some prayer from a trusted friend or church leader to help you in this. I believe that God will heal you in time, and help you to stop constantly revisiting those painful places. Try to keep a godly perspective. Remember what He has already brought you through. Perhaps it's time to focus your heart on the future and stop looking back. Paul writes:

"I do have one compelling focus: I forget all of the past as I fasten my heart to the future instead" (Philippians 3:13, TPT).

Sometimes we can become so obsessed with and distracted by the past that we can miss out on all the good things God is longing to pour into our lives today. Don't let that be you. Don't allow past disappointments to lower your future expectations. God is the restorer of broken lives and dreams. Nothing is impossible for Him. He is able to turn around even the toughest of situations.

What if God wanted to do something really fresh and new in your life? While you're nursing past regrets and harbouring a desire to return to what you've lost, God may be trying to point you in a different, more exciting, direction. We must choose to trust Him.

Don't allow the curveball you've been thrown to stop you living the life God has granted you. I often remind myself that, despite the challenges we face, it is really good to be alive. There is so much to be thankful for, and so much to experience and enjoy on this incredible planet.

So make a choice to trust God and step into everything He has for you. He will not disappoint. There is a new life to be lived. There are new adventures to go on and new experiences to enjoy.

Refuse to take the easy option

I was without a job for fourteen months during the two UK lockdowns. This was the first time since leaving school at the age of sixteen that I had been unemployed. It hurt. My pride hurt. Our bank account hurt. Everything hurt.

Because the country was in lockdown there were very few openings available, then towards the end of that season pastorates became available. Some attractive opportunities were presented, and interviews took place, but none of them felt right. Imagine turning down several full-time job opportunities when you have very little income! One friend suggested I should just take on a church so I could get paid until something better turned up, but my personal integrity wouldn't allow that.

Trusting God while you wait may mean turning down attractive opportunities. However, this was my mantra: it has to be God! To be right for us, it had to be God. I refused to settle for something that wasn't God's clear will, and ultimately He blessed us for being patient and waiting for Him to open the right door.

Trust Him one day at a time

This seems a bit obvious, yet I have found it really helpful. During our long waiting period God taught me not to look too far ahead. I needed to trust Him one day at a time, and with every fresh challenge that came our way. It was a daily choice for me. When I had a bad day, when discouragement, anxiety, worry and fear overwhelmed me, I had to make the decision to put it behind me and start afresh the next day. We are humans, not robots, and in my experience there will occasionally be bad days. When these occur we need to dust ourselves down and get going again.

I chose not to look too far ahead and to focus on living one day at a time. Didn't Jesus say:

"Therefore do not worry about tomorrow, for tomorrow will worry about itself. Each day has enough trouble of its own" (Matthew 6:34).

And don't forget the words of a guy who had his fair share of I-don't-know-what-to-do moments. King David said:

"But I trust in you, Lord; I say, "You are my God." My times are in your hands" (Psalm 31:14-15).

This was what carried me through as I continued to pray, wait and trust.

Acknowledge your own weakness and depend on His immense power

When we feel weak and overwhelmed, and are faced with what appear to be insurmountable challenges, we have little choice but to depend fully on God and to trust Him for what we ourselves cannot do.

I'm so grateful for Paul's honesty when he declared the following, despite the many challenges he faced:

"But he said to me, 'My grace is sufficient for you, for my power is made perfect in weakness.' Therefore I will boast all the more gladly about my weaknesses, so that Christ's power may rest on me. That is why, for Christ's sake, I delight in weaknesses, in insults, in hardships, in persecutions, in difficulties. For when I am weak, then I am strong" (2 Corinthians 12:9-10).

What an incredible man Paul was. We are indebted to him in so many ways. With great humility he was willing to share that, just like you and me, he had days and seasons when he struggled, felt weak and needed God. I have found his words so helpful whenever I have struggled, and I have experienced great release and relief in acknowledging my own struggles and weaknesses before God, and with close friends (we need one another!). It is at these times that Christ's power rests on me in a depth of measure that I have never experienced before.

Trust God even when He appears to have let you down

"Hezekiah trusted in the Lord, the God of Israel. There was no one like him among all the kings of Judah, either before him or after him" (2 Kings 18:5).

The life of Hezekiah demonstrates that bad stuff sometimes happens to people who have faithfully trusted and served God:

"After all that Hezekiah had so faithfully done, Sennacherib king of Assyria came and invaded Judah. He laid siege to the fortified cities, thinking to conquer them for himself" (2 Chronicles 32:1).

This was a desperate situation for a king who had faithfully followed God. However, despite being thrown an unexpected curveball, Hezekiah trusted, prayed and waited for God to intervene:

"And the Lord sent an angel who destroyed the Assyrian army with all its commanders and officers. So Sennacherib was forced to return home in disgrace to his own land. And when he entered the temple of his god, some of his own sons killed him there with a sword" (2 Chronicles 32: 21, NLT).

Perhaps you feel disappointed or angry that you've trusted and served God faithfully, and that God has let you down. (*Thanks God, for the mess I've found myself in!*) Perhaps you blame Him for your current circumstances. Why did He allow you take that step? Why didn't he protect you? Why didn't He intervene? *Where were you, God, when I needed you the most?*

Somehow, we must learn to trust God no matter what our current circumstances look like. But how do we do that? I think it starts with us asking God to forgive us for blaming Him. We live in a fallen world, so things will not always go our way and we will suffer losses at times. We must recognise that we are living in the space between the arrival of the Kingdom of God (which began when Jesus lived on earth in human form), and it becoming fully present when He returns. Things aren't perfect on earth... otherwise it would be heaven!

We also need to acknowledge our own mistakes or poor decision-making. Sometimes we are the ones who are to blame for the situations we find ourselves in. And we may need to accept that life is a mystery at times. We may never get to know the why in the now, so it's best to let go of the past and move forward, with His help. Then ask Him to help you trust Him more every day, and to bring complete restoration to your life and situation.

Trust God despite what you see

"For we live by faith, not by sight" (2 Corinthians 5:7).

Last year I suddenly developed a skin lesion near my eye. It was covered in dry, cracked skin and would not heal. It looked dreadful, and after googling it (never the right thing to do, but if we're honest we all do it!) I was even more scared. Thankfully, my GP got me in quickly for specialist photos and then an appointment with a dermatologist, who said he thought it was either cancerous or precancerous. I had an almost immediate biopsy and then had to wait nearly eight weeks before discovering it was precancerous, and that with chemotherapy cream it would heal. Praise God!

Everything had been pointing to skin cancer, but thankfully it wasn't. Experiencing that situation made my heart go out to all those awaiting diagnostic results. It's a horrible period, but somehow we must choose to live by faith and not by sight, and to believe for the best. I had to make a decision every day (sometimes several times a day!) to trust God. I had to accept that even if it was the 'big C', I would trust Him to heal and deliver me. He is God. He can do anything. He specialises in the impossible.

Perhaps you're waiting for results as you read this. Can I encourage you to keep praying, believing and trusting God deeply as you await the results? It's not easy, as I discovered, but we have a Father who promises to sustain us through every dark and difficult situation. He is 'Immanuel' – God with us – and He is with you no matter what you're facing.

You may have received bad news from a consultant, but never forget that the God who reigns and rules can also overrule. I'm always encouraged by the story of Hezekiah's terminal diagnosis in 2 Kings 20, when I see how God intervened, healed him and added fifteen years to his life. He is the God who overrules.

Alternatively, you may be waiting for other circumstances to change, or for a breakthrough, or for a new door to open. Again, the challenge is to trust God, and to live by faith and not by sight.

Don't focus on what you can see, but remind yourself that God has a plan and better days lie ahead. He is constantly at work in the background, planning and preparing. Our problem is, we can't see what He is doing until He goes public, and then we're full of praise for His work in our lives. Let's be expectant that our Father will work for the good of those who love Him (see Romans 8:28).

Be the one who trusts!

Whatever you are facing right now, it will almost certainly be affecting those around you, and they will likely be struggling with it, too. They will be asking the same questions of God and their faith as you, so lead well. Demonstrate your trust in God. Encourage them to trust. Be the one in your family, marriage, college, workplace, business or church who speaks positively and with faith.

I remember bumping into my neighbour when the second lockdown was over and he said to me, "Simon, something you said months ago really helped me to keep going and get through the pandemic."

I was so encouraged by this and thought to myself, *What could I have said that was so profound and so incredibly spiritual that helped this man through the pandemic?* So, I asked him.

"You said, 'We will get through this!'" he replied.

Be the one who trusts God and clearly demonstrates it (yes, even on days when you don't feel faith-filled and are wondering where God is!). Be the one who, like David, declares:

"Yet I am confident I will see the Lord's goodness while I am here in the land of the living. Wait patiently for the Lord. Be brave and courageous. Yes, wait patiently for the Lord" (Psalms 27:13-14, NLT).

Trust Him in the transitional seasons

April is one crazy month in the UK! One moment the sun is shining and the next there are squally showers and hail. Then almost immediately the sun comes out again. The weather just can't make up its mind whether it wants to be winter or spring! During this month, the weather goes through a significant transitional period.

God is always (and already!) at work in our transitional seasons. Our problem is that we can't predict what is about to happen. Just like the unsettled weather during the spring equinox, these transitional seasons in our lives can be very unsettling.

I have experienced seasons where one day I know exactly what we should do and the next I have no idea. Just ask my wife! My spirit is all over the place. Julia even suggested to me one day that I was like the double-minded man in James:

"*Being* a double-minded man, unstable *and* restless in all his ways [in everything he thinks, feels, or decides]" (James 1:8, AMP).

The double-minded man has no idea what he wants. That was me! Restless, unsettled and almost (but not quite) unstable. I was driving Julia mad, but I knew there was something better ahead. I believe there are times in our lives when we *know* that we *know* that we *know* there is something worth waiting for up ahead. I sense, during these seasons, that God will create a restlessness in our spirits in order to prepare us for what is coming next.

During our in-between season, I experienced some restless, sleep-deprived nights as I tossed and turned, and tried to work out why I felt the way I did, what was going on and what the solution might be. Unfortunately, the result was not great clarity and understanding; I would simply wake up feeling even more tired, grumpy, restless and frustrated than the day before!

On one occasion I felt God say to me: "Like the Israelites, you're wandering in the desert, but the Promised Land awaits. This is not it. This is not the place to settle. You know that in your spirit. That's why you're restless. That's why you can't settle. It's the place to do my work, and to let me work on and in you. Allow me to prepare you for the Promised Land, and the Promised Land for you."

You are likely in a transitional season right now, and perhaps you're feeling restless and struggling to work out what is going on or what you should do next. Make a choice to place your hand in the hand of your Saviour, and allow Him to lead you into all that He has planned and prepared for you since the beginning of time.

Focus on the job in hand

I am so inspired by the life of Caleb. Here is a man who followed God wholeheartedly, but, due to the fearful responses of ten other people, was robbed of the opportunity to enter the Promised Land. Yet God saw his heart:

"But because my servant Caleb has a different spirit and follows me wholeheartedly, I will bring him into the land he went to, and his descendants will inherit it"

Caleb had to wait forty-five long years to enter the Promised Land and claim his inheritance in Hebron (see Joshua 14). Imagine that!

In fact, he was 85 years old when the opportunity finally arose. He said:

"Now then, just as the Lord promised, he has kept me alive for forty-five years since the time he said this to Moses, while Israel moved about in the wilderness. So here I am today, eighty-five years old! I am still as strong today as the day Moses sent me out; I'm just as vigorous to go out to battle now as I was then. Now give me this hill country that the Lord promised me that day. You yourself heard then that the Anakites were there and their cities were large and fortified, but, the Lord helping me, I will drive them out just as he said."

It's clear that he waited well during this period; that he refused to be dispirited or downcast. He remained devoted to God for the entire time, and he focused on the job in hand, which was to join his brothers in fighting for Israel and to complete the conquest of the Promised Land.

So I resolved that, rather than becoming frustrated and paralysed by my situation, I would keep my heart right and devote myself wholeheartedly to God. I would work hard and focus on doing what I'd always done. I would not sit on my hands and feel sorry for myself. I would retain my spiritual disciplines and complete what God had given me to do.

It's important to keep practising the spiritual disciplines that have brought you this far. Maintain your commitments to prayer, worship, fellowship, service, giving and reaching out to others. Be faithful to all that God has called you to. Do your very best. Ask yourself what God has called you to do right now and finish the job in hand.

The postscript to this is that, once Israel had completed the conquest, Joshua gave him what he had been promised:

"Then Joshua blessed Caleb son of Jephunneh and gave him Hebron as his inheritance. So Hebron has belonged to Caleb son of Jephunneh the Kenizzite ever since, because he followed the Lord, the God of Israel, wholeheartedly"

---

1. D. Mathis, 'Here I Raise My Ebenezer', Desiring God, 7 February 2019: (accessed 14 August 2023).

Chapter Nine

Trusting God is a lifelong journey

Trusting God is a lifelong journey, especially when we live in an environment in which people have massive trust issues with other people and with God. Just as we have to learn to trust others, we need to learn to trust God. That takes time, so don't be too hard on yourself if you're struggling. As I said earlier, you're in good company.

Having destroyed the prophets of Baal, Elijah struggled to trust God in his dealings with a mouthy queen and did a runner into the desert. Yet God still had a plan and a purpose for his life. Esther had to learn to trust God in the palace where God had placed her. Simon Peter didn't trust God when he denied Jesus three times, yet he was reinstated and preached the first early Church sermon, after which 3,000 people became believers. David learned to trust God when he fought the lion and the bear, and years later Goliath simply presented him with a larger target for his sling and stones!

David later declared:

"Some trust in chariots and some in horses, but we trust in the name of the Lord our God" (Psalms 20:7).

Trust is a journey, and if you're one of those people who is praying, waiting and trusting right now, please understand that this is a significant time for you. What you are experiencing may not be easy. You may feel anxious, fearful and frustrated. You may feel restless. Perhaps nothing appears to be changing. However, one thing is most certainly occurring: your trust in God is growing with every passing day. One day you may appreciate the faith-building value of this season, because one day God will challenge you to trust Him with something greater.

Here's the thing: God is looking for men and women He can really trust. We are entrusted with different things in different seasons of our lives. He is looking for people who will not quiver, shake and quit at the slightest challenge; people who will not fall at the first hurdle; men and women who have learned how to really trust Him. As Jeremiah reminds us:

"'If you have raced with men on foot and they have worn you out, how can you compete with horses? If you stumble in safe country, how will you manage in the thickets by the Jordan?'" (Jeremiah 12:5).

He may well be testing you because He sees what lies ahead, and wants you to be strong and ready to fulfil the plans and purposes He has for your life.

Keep going! Don't quit!

I never fail to be challenged by the incredible persecution God's people have endured throughout history. Many people have trusted God enough to endure all kinds of hideous physical, emotional and spiritual attacks, and somehow they endured.

The writer to the Hebrews wrote:

Therefore, since we are surrounded by such a great cloud of witnesses, let us throw off everything that hinders and the sin that so easily entangles. And let us run with perseverance the race marked out for us, fixing our eyes on Jesus, the pioneer and perfecter of faith. For the joy that was set before him he endured the cross, scorning its shame, and sat down at the right hand of the throne of God. Consider him who endured such opposition from sinners, so that you will not grow weary and lose heart. (Hebrews 12:1-3)

Whenever I read that passage, I have a sense that all those who have endured before us are out there somewhere cheering us on. I can almost see them in the clouds of heaven shouting out encouragement: "With God's help we endured, and you can too! Don't quit! Keep going!"

There may, of course, be occasions when it is right to quit. The danger for many of us, however, is that we quit too soon. Most of the people we might class as successful – in their career, business, ministry, music, the arts, sport, family life, etc. – are people who have struggled, faced challenges and failed many times, but they simply refused to quit. Something made them keep going. Perhaps you need to ask God to give you the strength not to quit, but to endure. Who knows what lies just around the corner?

Trust, even though...

"Even though I walk through the darkest valley, I will fear no evil, for you are with me; your rod and your staff, they comfort me" (Psalms 23:4).

I wonder what your "even though" is. David, who likely wrote this psalm in later life, was reflecting on his youthful experiences as a shepherd boy and applying what he had learned to his adult life. I'm sure he had experienced some curveballs and waded through disappointments, loss, grief and bereavement. I know that path well, having suffered the loss of six people close to me in the past three years – including my parents. It's a desperately dark valley to walk through. I miss them very much.

Whatever you're going through, there is no need to be fearful, because God is with you in your "even though". Just as the sheep were comforted and reassured by the familiar sounds of the shepherd's rod and staff, please be comforted by the knowledge that whatever you might face, and whatever you are walking through right now, the Good Shepherd is walking through it with you. And you will eventually come out the other side of that dark valley.

Here's the wonderful thing: on the days when things are really dark, the valley is closing in around us and we're really struggling to trust God, lacking any measure of faith, He remains faithful. I love this wonderful promise:

"If we are faithless, He remains faithful; He cannot deny Himself" (2 Timothy 2:13, NKJV).

It is a constant reminder that He is with me when the curveballs strike and when I travel through the darkest of valleys. It's not dependant on me, my faith or my feelings. He is with me, and He is with you, too.

Whatever the possible outcome, choose to trust!

I loved the stories about Daniel in the Bible when I was a kid. What an amazing book, filled with incredible stories of faith and trust. For me, one stands out above the rest: the story of Shadrach, Meshach and Abednego:

Shadrach, Meshach and Abednego replied to him, "King Nebuchadnezzar, we do not need to defend ourselves before you in this matter. If we are thrown into the blazing furnace, the God we serve is able to deliver us from it, and he will deliver us from Your Majesty's hand. But even if he does not, we want you to know, Your Majesty, that we will not serve your gods or worship the image of gold you have set up." (Daniel 3:16-18)

Wow! What incredible trust in God.

Like Shadrach, Meshach and Abednego, we must choose to trust God, even when faced with almost certain death. The truth is, what He doesn't rescue you from He will sustain you through. God was right there in the flames, in the form of Jesus, protecting and sustaining those incredible young men.

So choose to trust

Can I encourage you to trust God like those guys – whatever curveball you've been thrown and however bleak and impossible your situation looks? Choose to trust God completely. Trust in Him for what you need today, tomorrow and beyond. Trust Him that your eternal destiny and those you love are in His hands. He can be trusted.

No matter what you can see, feel or sense. No matter how it looks. No matter how badly you've messed up. No matter the pain and trauma. No matter how stuck you are. No matter how impossible it looks. No matter the challenges. No matter the wolves at the door. No matter how long you've waited. No matter how much you've prayed. No matter how discouraged you are. No matter what God is doing in other people's lives. No matter what others are saying. No matter what has happened before. No matter what experience tells you. No matter all your doubts, anxieties and fears. No matter what – choose to trust. For the living God Himself is with you and for you, and not against you. Put your trust in Him.

"But blessed are those who trust in the Lord and have made the Lord their hope and confidence. They are like trees planted along a riverbank, with roots that reach deep into the water. Such trees are not bothered by the heat or worried by long months of drought. Their leaves stay green, and they never stop producing fruit" (Jeremiah 17:7-8, NLT).

Prayer

Father, thank you that You see me, love me and understand me, and that You care about what I'm going through. Help me to trust You deeply as I navigate this challenging season. Help me to trust You, no matter what my life looks like right now. May I live by faith, not by sight.

Help me to grieve my losses properly, and if there is any residual anger, bitterness, hurt, resentment or unforgiveness towards anyone, please forgive me and heal my heart.

Help me to experience a deep sense of Your love, joy and peace, and to have the patience, strength and courage to keep going... one day at a time. Enable me to look forward rather than back, and please fill my heart with hope for the future You have planned and purposed for me.

Help me to recognise Your still, small voice when You speak. Give me wisdom to make the right decisions rather than leaning on my own limited understanding. Help me not to strive to make things happen, but to wait patiently for You to intervene in my circumstances. You are the One who opens doors that no one else can shut. You are the God of miracles who rescues, restores and rebuilds broken lives.

Father, please increase my trust in You and help me to trust You more each day, as I continue to see Your plans and purposes being worked out in my life and in the lives of those around me. Amen

Discussion questions for small groups

Have you experienced times when God has allowed a massive curveball to impact your life? What happened? How did you get through that season?

Do you think you have grieved your losses properly?

What does everyday trust look like to you?

Which particular Bible verses have helped you trust God more? Are there any biblical promises you stand on when you particularly need to trust Him?

Have you been given any specific promises from God that you'd like to share?

How do you trust God when he appears to have gone silent and nothing appears to be changing?

Ask each person in the group for one area in which they need to trust God more, then pray for one another.

Part Four

"In the morning, Lord, you hear my voice; in the morning I lay my requests before you and wait expectantly." (Psalms 5:3)

Chapter Ten

Expect

The rallying cry of several English newspapers during the 2006 football World Cup in Germany was "England expects!" Football in its modern format was created in England, and the country hosts one of the most competitive football leagues in the world. Yet, since the inception of the World Cup in the 1930s, the England team has only won the tournament once.

That rallying call to the England team came from the words of Admiral Horatio Nelson on the eve of the Battle of Trafalgar on 21 October 1805. He sent a signal from HMS *Victory* declaring: "England expects that every man will do his duty."[1]

Trafalgar was the decisive naval engagement of the Napoleonic Wars, and it gave the UK control over the seas, further removing any possibility of a French invasion and conquest of Britain. The significance of the victory, and of the loss of Nelson during the battle, led to the phrase becoming embedded in the English psyche, and it has been regularly quoted, paraphrased and referenced up to the modern day... especially when England are playing!

Nelson expected his men to do their job and for victory to be theirs. As I considered his words, it occurred to me just how powerful a declaration it was. There was little, if any, doubt in Nelson's mind that the French would be defeated or that England would rule the waves.

As we come to the conclusion of this book, I want to encourage you to remain expectant. We do not place our faith and hope in men, nor in horses and chariots, as David described in Psalms 20:7, but in the Creator, Ruler and Sustainer of the universe. Our hope is found in God Himself.

Elijah expected rain!

Elijah is one of my favourite Old Testament characters. He made a name for himself by declaring that there would be no rain. There is no introduction or background story – just a guy who appears before Ahab, the king:

"Now Elijah the Tishbite, from Tishbe in Gilead, said to Ahab, 'As the Lord, the God of Israel, lives, whom I serve, there will be neither dew nor rain in the next few years except at my word'" (1 Kings 17:1).

This did not please the evil, idol-worshipping Israelite king, Ahab. However, Elijah was proved right! There was no rain for three years and a severe famine followed. Then, having been told by God that rain was on its way, Elijah had no doubt at all that it would come. Let's pick up the narrative here:

Then Elijah said to Ahab, "Go get something to eat and drink, for I hear a mighty rainstorm coming!" So Ahab went to eat and drink. But Elijah climbed to the top of Mount Carmel and bowed low to the ground and prayed with his face between his knees. Then he said to his servant, "Go and look out toward the sea." The servant went and looked, then returned to Elijah and said, "I didn't see anything." Seven times Elijah told him to go and look. Finally the seventh time, his servant told him, "I saw a little cloud about the size of a man's hand rising from the sea." Then Elijah shouted, "Hurry to Ahab and tell him, 'Climb into your chariot and go back home. If you don't hurry, the rain will stop you!'" And soon the sky was black with clouds. A heavy wind brought a terrific rainstorm, and Ahab left quickly for Jezreel. Then the Lord gave special strength to Elijah. He tucked his cloak into his belt and ran ahead of Ahab's chariot all the way to the entrance of Jezreel." (1 Kings 18:41-46, NLT)

Elijah fully expected rain. He prayed, waited and trusted. He had no doubt that God's word would come to pass. He had also expected the fire of God when he confronted the prophets of Baal before all Israel:

"Then the fire of the Lord fell and burned up the sacrifice, the wood, the stones and the soil, and also licked up the water in the trench" (1 Kings 18:38).

The fire God sent hadn't just burnt the sacrifice... it had obliterated everything!

Elijah was unlike many Western Christians, who often have a laissez-faire attitude when it comes to prayer. *Whatever will be, will be... If it's your will, Lord...* No. Elijah prayed earnestly and intensely, with absolute belief and expectation that the God who had answered with fire would answer with rain. Elijah expected rain. Seven times he asked his servant to go and check the horizon, until finally a small cloud the size of a man's hand appeared. Within minutes, the sky was heavy with rain-filled black clouds.

As we pray, as we wait, as we trust, we must believe and expect that at some point God will move and bring about the breakthrough. We must expect that a cloud the size of a man's hand will appear on the horizon. That the rains will come. That the fire will fall!

James later describes the incident as follows:

Tremendous power is released through the passionate, heartfelt prayer of a godly believer! Elijah was a man with human frailties, just like all of us, but he prayed and received supernatural answers. He actually shut the heavens over the land so there would be no rain for three and a half years! Then he prayed again, and the skies opened up over the land so that the rain came again and produced the harvest. (James 5:16-18, TPT)

Elijah was a man just like us, with all the same human frailties. Yet when he prayed, he believed he would receive what he had asked for in prayer (as Jesus instructs us to do in Matthew 21:22). You, too, can pray, wait, trust and be expectant, like Elijah.

When God says 'wait', we should hear 'expect'

Expectation is an essential characteristic for those who are praying, waiting and trusting. When David wrote the aforementioned Psalm 5:3, he recorded how he would lay his requests before God each morning and then wait expectantly for Him to act. The phrase often translated as "wait expectantly" is the Hebrew word *tsaphah*, which means "to look out or about, spy, keep watch", or to "watch expectantly".[2]

David wasn't passive in his praying and waiting. He anticipated that the Lord would show him mercy based on his personal revelation of who God was. He actively waited in expectation for God's intervention.

The psalmist sums it up well:

"I wait [patiently] for the Lord, my soul [expectantly] waits, And in His word do I hope" (Psalms 130:5, AMP).

Let us be people who wait expectantly.

George Müller

George Müller was an incredible man of faith. Having seen the plight of local orphans in the area, he set up an orphanage to meet their needs. Over the last couple of hundred years, thousands of children have not just benefited from the food, shelter and care he set up; they have also been introduced to faith in Jesus.

Müller completely trusted God for everything. He refused to take a stipend or make appeals. Rather, he chose to trust God for everything he needed. One incident is recorded in the early days of running the first orphanage he set up:

"The children are dressed and ready for school. But there is no food for them to eat," the housemother of the orphanage informed George Mueller. George asked her to take the 300 children into the dining room and have them sit (and wait!) at the tables. He thanked God for the food and waited. George knew God would provide food for the children as he always did. Within minutes, a baker knocked on the door. "Mr. Mueller," he said, "last night I could not sleep. Somehow, I knew that you would need bread this morning. I got up and baked three batches for you. I will bring it in."

Soon, there was another knock at the door. It was the milkman. His cart had broken down in front of the orphanage. The milk would spoil by the time the wheel was fixed. He asked George if he could use some free milk. George smiled as the milkman brought in ten large cans of milk. It was just enough for the 300 thirsty children.[3]

Müller sat the children down, ready to eat, while he waited and trusted God to provide. He fully expected Him to do so, and God never let him down. I can honestly say that He has never let me down either.

"I was young and now I am old, yet I have never seen the righteous forsaken or their children begging bread" (Psalms 37:25).

Be expectant!

Let me encourage you to be expectant as you read this final chapter. It is important to pray, wait and trust, but we must also remain expectant that God will intervene and turn our situations around.

I mentioned earlier that Jesus used the parable of the persistent widow to encourage the disciples to pray. Right at the end of his teaching, he says this:

"And the Lord said, 'Listen to what the unjust judge says. And will not God bring about justice for his chosen ones, who cry out to him day and night? Will he keep putting them off? I tell you, he will see that they get justice, and quickly. However, when the Son of Man comes, will he find faith on the earth?'" (Luke 18:6-8).

Jesus is talking about his return here, but the context relates to prayer and waiting for justice. He doesn't just want his people to pray, wait and trust; He wants us to demonstrate faith, to be expectant. So keep praying. Don't quit. Miracles happen every day, so never stop believing. God can change things very quickly in your life. Watch out for the cloud the size of a man's hand.

Remember, too, that God longs to be gracious to us. Isaiah declares:

"Therefore the Lord waits [expectantly] and longs to be gracious to you, And therefore He waits on high to have compassion on you. For the Lord is a God of justice; Blessed (happy, fortunate) are all those who long for Him [since He will never fail them]" (Isaiah 30:18, AMP).

According to David, He is the God who "turns darkness my into light" (Psalms 18:28). We can enter a room that is completely dark, yet at the flick of the switch the darkness becomes light. This reminds me that, in a mere moment, God can change our situations around. It might be a phone call, a letter or an email... who knows? But your life can change at the flick of a switch. It may feel as if you've been waiting in the wilderness forever, wondering what on earth God is doing. But it can all change in a moment.

So be encouraged and expectant. God Himself waits expectantly. He longs to have compassion on and be gracious to you. So hang in there and expect that at any moment He will step in and bring the breakthrough you need.

---

1. J. Vincent et al, 'England expects: English newspapers' narratives about the English football team in the 2006 World Cup', International Review for the Sociology of Sport: (accessed 14 August 2023).

2. 'Tsaphah', Biblia Paralela: ; Bible Hub: (both accessed 14 August 2023).

3. 'George Mueller, Orphanages Built By Prayer' Christianity, 16 July 2010: (accessed 14 August 2023).

Chapter Eleven

Waiting expectantly

When I was a child we used to go on what seemed like incredibly long car journeys along the Fosse Way from the Midlands to the South coast in a yellow Robin Reliant three-wheeler van like the one from BBC comedy *Only Fools and Horses*! The journey was made worse by the fact that my Dad had converted the van into a car by way of a cheap plastic seat in the back that the three of us children had to sit on! It was hard plastic and very uncomfortable, and we literally felt every bump we went over. Going around corners on just three wheels was similar to the sensation of being on a roller coaster.

Those long, uncomfortable journeys were constantly interrupted by cries of, "Are we nearly there yet?" My parents would try everything from playing "I spy" to "How many tractors/coaches can you see?" to "Can you see the sea yet?" (which always struck me as slightly bizarre halfway through the Cotswolds!). Kids today have no idea what we had to suffer! To be honest, nothing really helped us through the long wait until we arrived at my grandparents' house.

So, what can we do in the waiting season? How can we remain expectant during the sometimes arduous wait?

Live in the present!

"'Forget the former things; do not dwell on the past. See, I am doing a new thing! Now it springs up; do you not perceive it? I am making a way in the wilderness and streams in the wasteland'" (Isaiah 43:18-19).

These are familiar words, I know (though they are always worth reading again and dwelling on!), but I guess we all, myself included, need reminding that we simply can't afford to keep looking back at what we've lost or missed out on. I'm aware that I've mentioned this already, but I want to reiterate the importance of leaving the past behind and living in the present day. The temptation is always to keep rehearsing the disappointments and failures of the past season, but God wants us to put the past behind us and live in the present day, with its vast opportunities. Julia and I could easily have fallen foul of this after the bad experience at our previous church, but we refused to allow ourselves to go there. The truth is, we will miss so much of what God is doing today if we insist on living in yesterday.

As Psalm 118: 24 says, "this is the day that the Lord has made. We *will* rejoice and be glad in it!" We must make the most of every new day, recognising it as a gift from God.

Remember that God hasn't forgotten you

Speaking about the restoration of Israel, God declares:

"'Can a mother forget the baby at her breast and have no compassion on the child she has borne? Though she may forget, I will not forget you!'" (Isaiah 49:15).

This same truth applies to you and me. Though it may appear as if God has withdrawn from or forgotten us at times, this simply isn't true. God is with us in the wait. He will never leave us or abandon us.

"Be strong and courageous. Do not be afraid or terrified because of them, for the Lord your God goes with you; he will never leave you nor forsake you" (Deuteronomy 31:6).

The promise that was originally given to Joshua is repeated in multiple books of the Old and New Testament. His promise to you today is this: "I have not forgotten you, and I will never forsake you."

Maintain your confidence in Him

"I remain confident of this: I will see the goodness of the Lord in the land of the living. Wait for the Lord; be strong and take heart and wait for the Lord" (Psalms 27:13-14).

Life can feel really overwhelming at times. I have no idea what you're facing right now. You may be going through a really dark and challenging season. There may be numerous things kicking off at once (as if one curveball wasn't enough!). The pressure increases even more when you're responsible for the rent or mortgage payments, putting fuel in your car and food on the table for your family, paying bills or university fees, or preparing for retirement. The cost-of-living crisis hasn't helped, and it is even worse for those who are suffering with ill health or are unemployed.

What can you do and where can you turn? When fleeing from his son Absalom, David is thought to have written these words:

"My soul, wait thou only upon God; For my expectation is from him. He only is my rock and my salvation: he is my defence; I shall not be moved. In God is my salvation and my glory: the rock of my strength, and my refuge, is in God. Trust in him at all times; ye people, pour out your heart before him: God is a refuge for us. Selah" (Psalm 62:5-8, KJV).

Where does your confidence lie? In others, in your own abilities, in your bank balance, in the economy improving, or in a new job, pay rise or relationship? David's hope was in something more certain. His confidence was in the faithful, unchanging God we also serve. His expectation was that the God who had come through for him against the lion, the bear, Goliath and Saul, wasn't about to let him down now.

So don't focus on what you *don't* have right now. Don't focus on what you're waiting for. Focus on the One who is with you and put your confidence in Him.

"What, then, shall we say in response to these things? If God is for us, who can be against us? He who did not spare his own Son, but gave him up for us all – how will he not also, along with him, graciously give us all things?" (Romans 8:31-32).

Practise contentment

We live in an age where we are bombarded with advertisements and social media images of other people's lives. It's little wonder that we become discontented with our own lives, yet in reality we have so much. During the waiting season, practise being content with what

God has already given you. In fact, take time to value and appreciate what you have right now.

Paul said:

"I know what it is to be in need, and I know what it is to have plenty. I have learned the secret of being content in any and every situation, whether well fed or hungry, whether living in plenty or in want. I can do all this through him who gives me strength" (Philippians 4:12-13).

And the writer of Hebrews adds to this:

"Keep your lives free from the love of money and be content with what you have, because God has said, 'Never will I leave you; never will I forsake you'" (Hebrews 13:5).

So be content with and thankful for what you have, rather than disappointed by what you lack. There are so many people who have much less than you, and many who are enduring great suffering around the world.

Enjoy the journey

One of the happiest memories I have of our waiting season was seeing my grandson Archie splashing his hands in our birdbath at the end of the garden. A happy little two-year-old having a ball and getting absolutely soaked. I often watch the video of this, which we posted on social media. He was completely lost in the moment, and his face is a picture of unbridled joy and happiness.

It reminded me that as adults we take life far too seriously, and that even while we're in the waiting season we must remember to enjoy the journey and find things to laugh about. Laughter is good for the soul!

"A happy heart is good medicine and a joyful mind causes healing, But a broken spirit dries up the bones" (Proverbs 17:22, AMP).

Julia and I became aware that we needed to choose joy while we waited for God to intervene in our situation, so we chose to watch some old comedy shows on TV. We almost forced ourselves to create fun and laughter in our house. We had become too serious and needed some joy for the journey we were on. We laughed a lot (yes, a lot!) during our in-between season, and it did our spirits good.

Nehemiah reminds us that: "The joy of the Lord is your strength" (Nehemiah 8:10).

Whatever you are facing right now, and however long it has been going on, let me encourage you not to allow the seriousness of your situation to remove every trace of joy from your life. The great apostle Paul, who himself faced so much persecution and so many challenges, said:

Be cheerful with joyous celebration in every season of life. Let your joy overflow! And let gentleness be seen in every relationship, for our Lord is ever near. Don't be pulled in different directions or worried about a thing. Be saturated in prayer throughout each day, offering your faith-filled requests before God with overflowing gratitude. Tell him every detail of your life, then God's wonderful peace that transcends human understanding, will guard your heart and mind through Jesus Christ. Keep your thoughts continually fixed on all that is authentic and real, honorable and admirable, beautiful and respectful, pure and holy, merciful and kind. And fasten your thoughts on every glorious work of God, praising him always. (Philippians 4:4-8, TPT)

Be the most positive person in the room

There were times during our in-between season, especially early on, when I was incredibly discouraged, miserable and difficult to live with. It was an incredibly challenging period for us both.

As is so often the case, God challenged me about my attitude and said that – despite everything we were going through, and with His help – He wanted me to be "the most positive guy in the room". To trust Him and be an example to others in this.

He wanted me to choose life, not death; faith, not fear; victory, not defeat; courage, not discouragement; joy, not despair. He wanted me to look forward and not back. And with God's help, this is what I did.

When we walk in faith and victory we can change the atmosphere around us, despite everything we're facing. While you wait, be the most positive person in the room. Remember that you are on the winning side, in fact – because you have God on your side.

Hold on to hope!

"Let us hold unswervingly to the hope we profess, for he who promised is faithful" (Hebrews 10:23).

It was Dame Deborah James who coined the phrase "rebellious hope" to highlight her absolute determination to beat bowel cancer and not allow it to control her life. Even though she was going through a horrendous battle, she urged others to never give up, to live life to the fullest and to check their poo! What an incredible example of somebody holding on to hope.

While you wait and trust God, make sure you hold on to hope. Be almost rebellious in your hoping.

Keep your focus on God and absolutely refuse to allow other people, your circumstances or your feelings to bring you down, steal your joy or destroy your hope. The Word of God encourages us to hold on to hope. As I've said before, better days almost certainly lie ahead. The psalmist writes:

"We wait in hope for the Lord; he is our help and our shield. In him our hearts rejoice, for we trust in his holy name. May your unfailing love be with us, Lord, even as we put our hope in you" (Psalm 33:20-22).

And in Micah we read:

"But as for me, I watch in hope for the Lord, I wait for God my Saviour; my God will hear me" (Micah 7:7).

Never allow the disappointment of the past to diminish your hope and expectation of a brighter future. Demonstrate faith, for God is with you. He is your rock and your salvation. He is your hope.

As Paul reminds us:

"For in this hope we were saved. But hope that is seen is no hope at all. Who hopes for what they already have? But if we hope for what we do not yet have, we wait for it patiently" (Romans 8:24-25).

Don't lose heart!

"Therefore we do not lose heart. Though outwardly we are wasting away, yet inwardly we are being renewed day by day. For our light and momentary troubles are achieving for us an eternal glory that far outweighs them all. So we fix our eyes not on what is seen, but on what is unseen, since what is seen is temporary, but what is unseen is eternal" (2 Corinthians 4:16-18).

As the wait goes on, it can be easy to look at our circumstances and lose heart, allowing discouragement to start knocking at the door. It can be tempting quit, but don't give up or you may miss out. Do not allow yourself to miss out through lack of faith.

In these moments I've discovered that I need to have a word with myself, and apparently I'm in good company:

"So I say to my soul, 'Don't be discouraged. Don't be disturbed. For I know my God will break through for me.' Then I'll have plenty of reasons to praise him all over again. Yes, he is my saving grace!" (Psalms 42:11, TPT).

Joshua needed several reminders to be strong and courageous. I'm sure he trusted God deeply and was expectant that God would bring him great victories as they entered the Promised Land, but he still had to fight off fear and discouragement. He had to learn to depend daily on God's strength and power.

As the psalmist declared:

"My strength is found when I wait upon you. Watch over me, God, for you are my mountain fortress; you set me on high!" (Psalms 59:9, TPT).

Don't try to get through this challenging season in your own strength. Just like Elijah, who needed food and rest on Mount Horeb (see 1 Kings 19), you'll need strength and sustenance for the journey ahead.

Don't lose heart while you wait. Instead, ask God for fresh strength, energy and courage each day. There is daily strength available for the waiting season. In order to access it, we need to go to the power source and sit in His presence, allowing ourselves to be strengthened and empowered by Him. Paul reminds us:

"Finally, be strong in the Lord and in his mighty power" (Ephesians 6:10).

Expect the unexpected

Tales of the Unexpected was an early 1980s British TV series based on the short stories of author Roald Dahl, which were either a touch sinister or had comedic undertones. Each episode had an expected twist at the end.

The Bible is also full of twists and turns. It looked as though David had lost everything at Ziklag (see 1 Samuel 30), and his men were ready to stone him. They had returned from battle to discover that the Amalekites had raided their camp, burned it and taken their wives, sons and daughters captive.

However, God encouraged David to pursue the raiding party, and there was an unexpected twist when they found an abandoned Egyptian – the slave of their enemies, the Amalekites – in a field. After providing him with food and refreshment, he led them to where their wives, families and possessions were. God used one of

David's enemies to restore everything to him and his men. In fact, the writer records:

"David recovered everything the Amalekites had taken, including his two wives. Nothing was missing: young or old, boy or girl, plunder or anything else they had taken. David brought everything back. He took all the flocks and herds, and his men drove them ahead of the other livestock, saying, 'This is David's plunder'" (1 Samuel 30:18-20).

The Lord works in mysterious ways! There have been so many times during my life and ministry when God has provided in unexpected ways and through unexpected people. On one occasion I was away on mission with the Bible college I was attending, and I'd been forced to leave Julia with very little food or money. The next day some friends from a church in the north of England turned up with a van filled with great food, which kept our whole family fed for days! It was completely unexpected and unannounced. Praise God.

God even used an undertaker!

Talking about Bible college, I remember how difficult our circumstances were when we were preparing to follow the call to ministry with our four children. We were in debt, had no money, no income, couldn't rent our home out and didn't even have the college fees, never mind the money to rent a home for ourselves. Looking back it was crazy, but we knew God had told us to go to college.

Out of the blue we received a phone call from a pastor friend (interestingly, at the exact moment we and our whole house group were praying for a home for us!). He had befriended an undertaker at his church in Cambridgeshire, and this guy just happened to have a small two-bedroomed house in Nantwich, where the college was.

It was what an estate agent would call a "two up, two down" house. My initial reaction was, "I don't think that would work. It only has two bedrooms and there are six of us!" However, Julia felt that, as we had literally been praying when the call came in, we should go and have a look.

A couple of weeks later the undertaker drove hundreds of miles to show us around his lovely little terraced house. He made us a nice meal and then, to our complete surprise, offered it to us rent-free for several months. We moved in shortly afterwards. It was a gift from God, and we made it work. A year or so later, God provided a three-bedroomed apartment on the beautiful college campus, which our kids loved. Isn't God good?

God met all our needs. It didn't look exactly the way we expected, but it was just what we needed. Don't discount someone or something out of hand because it isn't what you anticipated, but rather be open to God to meet your needs in whichever way He desires.

Make sure you're ready for the door to open!

The parable of the ten virgins (see Matthew 25) reminds us that we need to be ready for the door to open. In the case of the five foolish virgins who weren't ready for the door to be opened, who weren't ready to meet the bridegroom, the door was firmly shut. Worse still, the bridegroom replied that he didn't even know them.

I've always found the story of how Abraham sent his servant Eliezer to find a wife for his son Isaac (see Genesis 24), from among his own people, a bit of a mystery. It's a beautiful story of God's guiding hand in bringing together two people who were to be central to the story of Israel. But why would a woman suddenly decide to up sticks, leave her family behind and marry a guy she had never even met? It's a bit like the TV show *Married at First Sight*. Now, I understand Eastern traditions and arranged marriages, but, after taking Eliezer home to meet her family and explain what had happened, and even after being encouraged to stay for the customary ten days and say her fond farewells, Rebekah agreed to go immediately.

What seems clear to me is that God had somehow prepared her for this moment. He had been watching young Rebekah. He had studied her attitude and her actions. He knew she was willing to serve others. She not only provided Eliezer with a drink, but also offered to water his ten thirsty camels. Camels drink a lot of water. In fact, they can drink up to twenty gallons at a time!

Great doors will open for those who are willing to serve faithfully in the small, daily tasks and in the least glamorous aspects of life. Rebekah was ready when the door opened. I suspect she had been praying, waiting and trusting that God had a husband lined up for her. Her response suggests as much. "'I will go,' she said" (Genesis 24:58). She had been waiting expectantly and was ready when the moment arrived.

When God opens the door and says, "Go!", we must be ready to obey him. We must be ready to ignore our fears, refuse to downplay our gifts and abilities, accept that there may be challenges, and step through the door to move in the direction He is leading us in. I remember my mother saying to me, after we had decided to go to Bible college and were facing many challenges and problems, that this was a good sign. In fact, she said she would have been concerned if everything was going smoothly, because following Jesus is never straightforward or easy. The pathway is often narrow and immensely challenging.

When things change, when God steps in, will you be ready? Is there anything you should be doing today to ensure that you're absolutely ready to go when God moves? What if the door opened tomorrow? Would you be ready? Is there anything you need to do to prepare? Do you need to get fit, lose weight, create some new habits, change your attitude, stop sinning, declutter, study, clear your debts or put your house in order? Just like the ten virgins, it is your responsibility to be ready when the door finally opens.

Why not ready yourself to try something new? Why not believe for the unbelievable? The door that's about to open may lead you into something completely new and different from anything you've done before. Don't miss it! Let's stop playing it safe and trying to foresee each step of the journey before we have taken the first step. Let's choose to step across the threshold into all that God has for us.

The wait will be worth it!

"This vision is for a future time. It describes the end, and it will be fulfilled. If it seems slow in coming, wait patiently, for it will surely take place. It will not be delayed" (Habakkuk 2:3, NLT).

I can still remember the joy Julia and I felt when our first daughter was born, and then the second... and years later our grandchildren. Each time, we spent nine months praying, waiting and trusting God, and then we got to meet a new family member for the very first time. These were precious, unforgettable moments.

I also remember buying my first car (a clapped-out, just about roadworthy orange Mini!), our wedding day, our first home, the first time we visited America, meeting my birth parents for the first time, walking my daughters down the aisle (the greatest privilege for any father), holding the first book I had ever written in my hand, getting the keys to our new church buildings... the list goes on. Each time, the wait was truly worth it. In fact, the best things in life are usually worth waiting for.

As I look back on my life, I can see many deeply challenging moments and dark seasons of the soul: illness, grief, loss, attacks, rejection, betrayal, unexplained difficulties, troubles, frustrations, anxieties and fears. I can also see that there have been countless divinely appointed times and seasons, God-scheduled events and appointments, all of which were part of His perfect and unique plan for my life. Nobody can stop God's plans and purposes from coming to pass. There is a deep sense of peace in knowing that.

You may be in a season of darkness and turmoil at the moment. You may feel completely stuck. You may be in a season of waiting. You may be bursting to see the promises and purposes of God fulfilled in your life. You may even feel that you're ready. The truth is, God won't move until He's sure you're prepared for what is coming next. His timing is always perfect.

I would add that when God plants a dream or desire in your heart, that's the easy bit. What often follows are obstacles, challenges, attacks, tests, trials, self-doubt and often a period of waiting, when little appears to happen. In my experience, God-planted desires often arrive well in advance of their realisation, and sometimes we must wait way longer than we ever anticipated. Vision must always await God's appointed time.

Expect!

During our fourteen-month period of praying, waiting and trusting, I recorded one of my conversations with God in my journal. I hope it encourages you, as you continue to pray, wait and trust.

I said to God:

We just feel stuck. Not able to move forward or go back. We're just plain stuck. Held fast by the Almighty, who knows the plans He has for us. I just wish You'd let us know. This season, preordained as I believe it was, has lasted nearly a year. You've provided. You've carried. You've enabled us to get through, but we've both experienced so many down days and flat days. Life carries on for everyone else and we remain stuck. Thank God that things can change in a moment. You are the God who turns darkness into light. I just wish you would, Lord – today! It's excruciating. We're stuck and we're not going to become unstuck until You speak the Word, and we are released from this wilderness. Until You open the door, it remains shut.

And my Father replied:

What if this long wait has been all about My timing and My positioning in order to grant you the desires and secret petitions of your heart? You have spent your life trusting and delighting yourself in Me. What if My reward is coming? What if I am going to grant you your heart's desire? What if My plans for you are to really prosper you and not harm you, and to give you a hope and a future? What if I am about to restore the many years the locust has stolen from you? What if I am about to raise you up before men in a way you never anticipated or expected? What if I am going to provide a feast in the midst of your enemies? What if I am going to do immeasurably more than you could ever ask, dream or imagine?

Wouldn't that be worth the wait?

Wouldn't that be worth praying, waiting and trusting for?

Prayer

Father, I want to place my life in Your hands again today. Everything feels like it is up in the air right now. I feel stuck. I have no idea what the future holds, but I'm grateful that I know the One who holds my future. Thank you that I can place my trust in You, today and every day.

Thank you that You haven't forgotten me. Help me to keep my eyes fixed on You, to keep my hope and confidence in you, and to be content with all that I have right now in this season of my life. Help me to be strong and courageous, and never to lose heart. May my home be filled with positivity, joy and laughter.

Help me not just to be a person who is willing to PRAY, WAIT and TRUST, but also to be someone who is full of expectation. May the unexpected happen during this next season. Help me to be ready and prepared, like Rebekah, for when you move.

And may I continue to know the peace of God that passes all understanding. May it saturate my heart and mind, and may I experience Your wonderful provision in this challenging season in every sense. For Your glory. Amen

A final thought...

I'm praying for everyone who reads this, and who is struggling in this season, that the incredible peace of God will fill your hearts and minds in Christ Jesus (see Philippians 4:7), and that one day soon you will be able to say with me:

"In that day they will say, 'Surely this is our God; we trusted in him, and he saved us. This is the Lord, we trusted in him; let us rejoice and be glad in his salvation'" (Isaiah 25:9).

Be blessed!

Simon

Discussion questions for small groups

What has stood out to you most from this chapter?

What do you think you should add to your walk with God?

What can we learn from the life of Elijah?

Why was Elijah so confident that God would answer his prayers?

Share a time in your life that you have known, beyond doubt, that God would intervene or answer your prayers. Explain why you were so confident.

Has God ever answered your prayers in an unexpected way?

What is your general attitude to praying, and what can we learn about prayer from James 5:16-18?

Do you expect God to answer your prayers? Do you ever give up too easily?

How can we live more expectantly?

As you reflect on this teaching series, which area do you need to focus on most? Pray, wait, trust... or expect? Explain why.

Do you know this God?

The apostle Paul declares:

"It's in Christ that we find out who we are and what we are living for. Long before we first heard of Christ and got our hopes up, he had his eye on us, had designs on us for glorious living, part of the overall purpose he is working out in everything and everyone" (Ephesians 1:11-12, MSG).

If this is true, our days of searching to fill that hole inside of us are over. We have found what we are looking for: a personal relationship with the creator of the universe. It is astounding to think that God saw us before we were even born; that He had His eye on us and, more than that, had an incredible plan and purpose for our lives.

Perhaps you haven't connected with God yet. If not, He wants to reveal Himself to you as your heavenly Father. He loves you. He sees you. He has a wonderful plan and purpose for your life. He is the God who brings hope, restoration, peace and healing. He is the One who restores courage to the most discouraged.

If you'd like to know Him for yourself, all you have to do is invite Him into your life. You're really just saying yes to the King of the universe. You can do that by praying this simple prayer, and I promise that He will accept you:

Father God, I come to You today. I don't know everything about You, but I know that I need You in my life. Please forgive me for all the things I've done wrong and wipe the slate of my past clean. I need a new start today. I'm choosing to trust You, and I gladly surrender my life to You. Take me just as I am, and come and live inside me through Your Holy Spirit. Amen

If you prayed that prayer, you have just become a Christian. Welcome to the family of God! The next thing you need to do is find a lively, Bible-believing church and start attending. Speak to the leaders and tell them what has happened. If you need help with this, please don't hesitate to contact me via the email address below and I'll help you find a good church in your area. If you don't feel ready to pray yet then can I encourage you to keep exploring the Christian faith. One way in which you can do this is to join a local Alpha course. You can find more details at alpha.org

God bless you!

Simon

Feedback

I'd love to hear your feedback on this book or, even better, to see your review on Amazon, Goodreads or wherever you purchased it.

Email

If you have any comments or suggestions, or have noticed any typos, please email me at revlawton@gmail.com

Further reading

You can read more of my thoughts at simonlawton.com

Connect

Join me on X (formerly Twitter), Facebook and Instagram: simonlawton

If you've enjoyed reading this book, you may also enjoy Simon's first book, entitled *Imagine: Trusting God Like Never Before*. Imagine what your life would be like if you really trusted God. Imagine the impact on your faith, your family and your other relationships. Imagine the impact on your career, ambitions, dreams, finances and health. Imagine the doors God might open and the new adventures you might enjoy. Imagine the lasting legacy you might leave for the generations to come.

So many of us struggle to trust God, yet this is the key to discovering the life He intended for us. Using Proverbs 3:5-6 as a core text, Simon will take you on a journey of new faith and discovery. If we learn to trust God like never before, we will begin to live like never before! *Imagine* is available from Amazon and other major online bookshops.

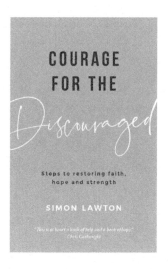

We live in such challenging days – so many are struggling with stress, anxiety & fears, and are wondering how they will get through everything they face. The five Ds – discouragement, disappointment, disillusionment, despondency and despair – are very real. All of us experience these feelings at one time or another, but many feel overwhelmed by them.

So how do we combat these feelings and how can we develop courage when we are struggling? Simon Lawton explores these questions and offers many helpful, Bible-based solutions. This thirty day devotional book will help you walk in renewed faith and increased strength, despite your circumstances. Purchase *"Courage for the discouraged"* now and immediately begin to discover fresh hope and strength as you move from discouragement to courage TODAY! It's available from Amazon and other major online bookshops.

THE
END
OF THE
BEGINNING

A story of hope in the midst of grief and loss

Julia Lawton

Julia's life was unexpectedly turned upside down. Nigel, her previously fit and healthy husband, was admitted to hospital feeling unwell and three days later had passed away. Julia and her three little boys were suddenly and without warning left with no husband and daddy. Shocked, heartbroken, angry, fearful and numb, the pain and the grief of her loss was unbearable. It felt like the end and that her life was over. However - it was just the end of the beginning. A new chapter of her life was about to be written.

Julia tells her story of loss, grief and of finding faith for herself. She shares with great honesty and transparency the challenges of the journey, facing the stages of grief, re-marrying and becoming the person that God had called her to be. Julia's story will bring comfort, hope and encouragement to all those who have found themselves feeling that their lives have ended following the loss of a loved one. It's available from Amazon and other major online bookshops.

Printed in Great Britain
by Amazon

30187686R00096